AF705522

ENVIRONMENTAL FLOWS ASSESSMENT AND MANAGEMENT FOR ADB-FINANCED PROJECTS

GOOD PRACTICE NOTE

DECEMBER 2025

ASIAN DEVELOPMENT BANK

ADB

6 ADB Avenue, Mandaluyong City, 1550 Metro Manila, Philippines
Tel +63 2 8632 4444; Fax +63 2 8636 2444
www.adb.org

ISBN 978-92-9277-623-7 (print); 978-92-9277-624-4 (PDF); 978-92-9277-625-1 (e-book)
Publication Stock No. TIM250548-2
DOI: http://dx.doi.org/10.22617/TIM250548-2

Note:
In this publication, “$” refers to United States dollars.

Cover design by Edith Creus.

On the cover: Chea River, Guadalcanal, Solomon Islands (photo by Francesco Ricciardi).

Contents

Tables and Figures

TABLES

FIGURES

Acknowledgments

This Good Practice Note—Environmental Flows Assessment and Management for ADB-financed projects—was developed with leadership and technical guidance from Cate Brown (ADB Consultant at Southern Waters Ecological Research and Consulting, South Africa) and Lois Koehnken (ADB Consultant from Australia). Francesco Ricciardi (Senior Safeguards Specialist (Environment) from the Office of Safeguards, ADB) provided technical oversight, coordinated the preparation and peer review process, and provided strategic direction to align the guidance with ADB's Environmental and Social Framework and operational needs. We thank colleagues across ADB departments and resident missions for their thoughtful comments during drafting, pilot applications, and map/content clearances, and we appreciate the contributions of editors, designers, and administrative staff who supported production.

Abbreviations

AAF	average annual flow
ADB	Asian Development Bank
BBM	building block methodology
CASIMIR	Computer Aided Simulation Model for Instream Flow and Riparia
CIA	cumulative impact assessment
DRIFT	downstream response to imposed flows transformations
EFlows	environmental flows
EFMP	environmental flows management plan
ESIA	environmental and social impact assessment
GIS	geographic information system
HPP	hydroelectric power project
IFC	International Finance Corporation
MAR	mean annual runoff
TOR	terms of reference
UNEP	United Nations Environment Programme
WBG	World Bank Group
WCD	World Commission on Dams

Executive Summary

What Are EFlows?

Environmental flows (EFlows) are the quantity, timing, and quality of water, sediment, and biota flows needed to sustain healthy rivers, wetlands, estuaries, and the communities that depend on them. They help protect ecosystem services, biodiversity, and livelihoods while supporting sustainable development.

Purpose of This Guidance

This note supports Asian Development Bank (ADB) staff, borrowers, and partners in integrating EFlows into project planning, design, implementation, and monitoring. This guidance

(i) explains EFlows concepts and principles,
(ii) provides a step-by-step approach to setting and assessing EFlows,
(iii) offers guidance on integration into project development,
(iv) recommends monitoring and adaptive management strategies, and
(v) shares case studies and good practices.

Why EFlows Matter

Rivers face increasing pressure from infrastructure, urbanization, sediment extraction, and climate change. Altered flow regimes degrade habitats, reduce biodiversity, and harm livelihoods. EFlows help balance development with ecosystem health, supporting resilience and compliance with ADB's Environmental and Social Framework.

Key Elements of an EFlows Assessment

Effective EFlows assessments consider:

(i) **Hydrology and Hydraulics.** Seasonal flow patterns and ecological functions.
(ii) **Sediment Dynamics.** Maintaining channels and habitats.
(iii) **Water Quality.** Oxygen, nutrients, and pollutants.
(iv) **Connectivity.** Movement of water, sediment, and species.
(v) **Human Use.** Multiple pressures and cumulative impacts.

When Is an EFlows Assessment Needed?

An Eflows assessment is required for projects that may impact hydrology, hydraulics, sediment transport, water quality, and/or aquatic species connectivity, including dams, barrages, irrigation schemes, flood control structures, and urban developments.

Assessment Approach

(i) **Scope.** Consider upstream, in-channel, and downstream effects; use long-term data (>30 years) where possible.

(ii) **Resolution.** Tailor to project type, location, and sensitivity; avoid outdated rules (e.g., "10% flow").

(iii) **Method.** Use hydrological, hydraulic, habitat, holistic, or ecosocial modeling, with scenario analysis to explore trade-offs.

(iv) **Data Gaps.** Use local and/or traditional knowledge to supplement limited monitoring data.

Team and Process

EFlows assessments should be led by an experienced EFlows practitioner, supported by a multidisciplinary team, e.g., hydrologists, ecologists, and social scientists. Typical steps:

(i) Inception and review.

(ii) Scenario development.

(iii) Modeling and data collection.

(iv) Expert analysis and reporting.

(v) Stakeholder engagement.

(vi) Decision and target-setting.

(vii) Environmental Flows Management Plan (EFMP).

(viii) Monitoring and adaptive management.

Environmental Flows Management Plan

The EMFP formalizes the EFlows framework, including targets, roles for implementation, and procedures for monitoring, financing, and adaptive management

Monitoring and Adaptive Management

Begin pre-construction to establish a baseline; track compliance, ecological outcomes, and community feedback. Adjust strategies based on evidence to maintain project effectiveness and ecosystem resilience.

Special Considerations

The construction and commissioning phases require strict measures to avoid flow disruption, sediment release, habitat damage, and pollution. Protect tributaries and off-channel habitats as vital refuges for species.

1 Introduction

1.1 Background and Rationale

The Asian Development Bank (ADB) promotes environmentally sustainable development, focusing on environmental flows (EFlows) management in water resource projects to ensure river health is maintained despite infrastructure developments. Effective management of these flows is vital for preserving the ecological integrity of rivers, wetlands, and other aquatic ecosystems while ensuring the sustainability of water resources for diverse uses.

1.2 Purpose of the Guidance Note

This guidance note is intended to assist ADB staff and its borrowers/clients in including EFlows in the planning, design, implementation, and monitoring of ADB-supported water projects. It aims to:

(i) explain EFlows concepts, principles, and their role in sustainable water management;
(ii) provide a step-by-step approach to choosing a level of assessment, assessing, and setting EFlows for different types of water projects;
(iii) offer practical guidance for integrating EFlows throughout all stages of project development;
(iv) recommend monitoring and adaptive management strategies; and
(v) share case studies and good practices from EFlows implementation worldwide.

1.3 Definition of Environmental Flows

The ADB Environmental and Social Safeguard Framework (ADB 2024) defines EFlows as:

> "The quantity, timing and quality of the flow of water, sediment and biota necessary to sustain freshwater and estuarine ecosystems, and the human livelihoods and well-being that depend on these ecosystems"
>
> (World Bank Group [WBG] 2018; ADB 2024).

1.4 Importance of Environmental Flows

Rivers are natural freshwater channels that flow toward lower-lying bodies of water such as estuaries, oceans, or lakes. River ecosystems consist of flowing water, sediment transport, habitats, and the diverse plant and animal life that rely on them. These ecosystems are closely linked to and help sustain other aquatic environments, including wetlands and estuaries.

Rivers serve many essential functions for people: they generate energy, supply water for agriculture and industry, deliver construction materials like stones, gravel, and sand, sustain food and livelihoods, and support transportation, leisure, and recreation.

Human activities, such as constructing dams and reservoirs, extracting sediment, and expanding urban areas, alter the natural flow of water and sediments and obstruct the movement of aquatic species. Climate change further increases these pressures. Disruptions to natural river flow patterns can degrade ecosystems, threaten aquatic life, and reduce the ability to support human needs.

EFlows and their assessments help developers and other stakeholders understand how development affects rivers and provide guidance in mitigating and managing those impacts.

A good EFlows assessment considers the river's geology, flow patterns, the plants and animals it supports, and how people use the river for economic, social, and cultural purposes (Vos 2020). This understanding helps to find a balance between human water needs, the long-term health of rivers, and the communities that rely on them. It also helps developers and other stakeholders avoid unintended consequences resulting from their projects, manage risks fairly, avoid conflict, and ensure projects comply with environmental laws, thereby avoiding costly delays or redesigns.

Well-designed EFlows are widely used to support healthy rivers, wetlands, floodplains, and estuaries worldwide (e.g., European Water Framework Directive 2000). Their value in sustainable water management is well recognized (World Commission on Dams [WCD] 2000; Hobbs and Harris 2001; Baron et al. *2002), and most water professionals agree that EFlows are essential for sustainable water development (Kumar and Jayakumar 2020; Tickner et al. 2020).*

2 Key Aspects of an Environmental Flows Assessment

The assessment of EFlows is based on understanding the following (WWF 2017):

(i) The timing, pattern, and volume of the flow of water (hydrology), and how deep the water is, how fast it is flowing, and the parts of the river that are inundated (hydraulics).
(ii) The physical, biological, and chemical makeup of the water (water quality).
(iii) The shape and composition of river channels and the types of habitats they offer, and physical processes such as erosion and deposition of sediments (geomorphology).
(iv) The ecological functions and life cycles of the plants and animals that live in and around the river (biology).
(v) The movement of organisms, energy, and matter through a river system (connectivity).
(vi) The type and scale of human uses of the system and their impact on ecological functioning (human resource use).

2.1 Hydrology and Hydraulics

A river's natural flow patterns change with the seasons, creating a variety of flow events throughout the year. For instance (WWF 2017):

(i) Floods during the wet season fill wetlands and floodplains, carry sediments and nutrients, shape habitats, and refresh shallow river channels.
(ii) Spates, which typically occur in the transitional seasons (spring and autumn), trigger breeding and movement in animals and plants.
(iii) Low flows in the dry season support plant growth and allow farming on riverbanks, but they also bring tough conditions, increasing competition for water between ecosystems and people.

The onset and duration of each season coincide with other environmental changes, such as changes in ambient water temperatures that trigger biological functions, including egg development, growth, or the emergence of insect larvae. These seasonal variations, combined with broader climate patterns that bring wetter or drier years, create a dynamic environment that supports different species at different times, preventing any one species from dominating and helping to maintain biodiversity.

Changes to these patterns can affect the whole river ecosystem and other ecosystems connected to it. For instance, dams and reservoirs typically reduce wet season flows, including floods, and release water during the dry season. This changes the volume of water in the river and "flattens out" the river's natural flow patterns, changing the timing and duration of the seasons (Figure 1).

Figure 1: Example of Changes in Timing and Volumes of the Flow of Water with an In-Channel Dam and Reservoir

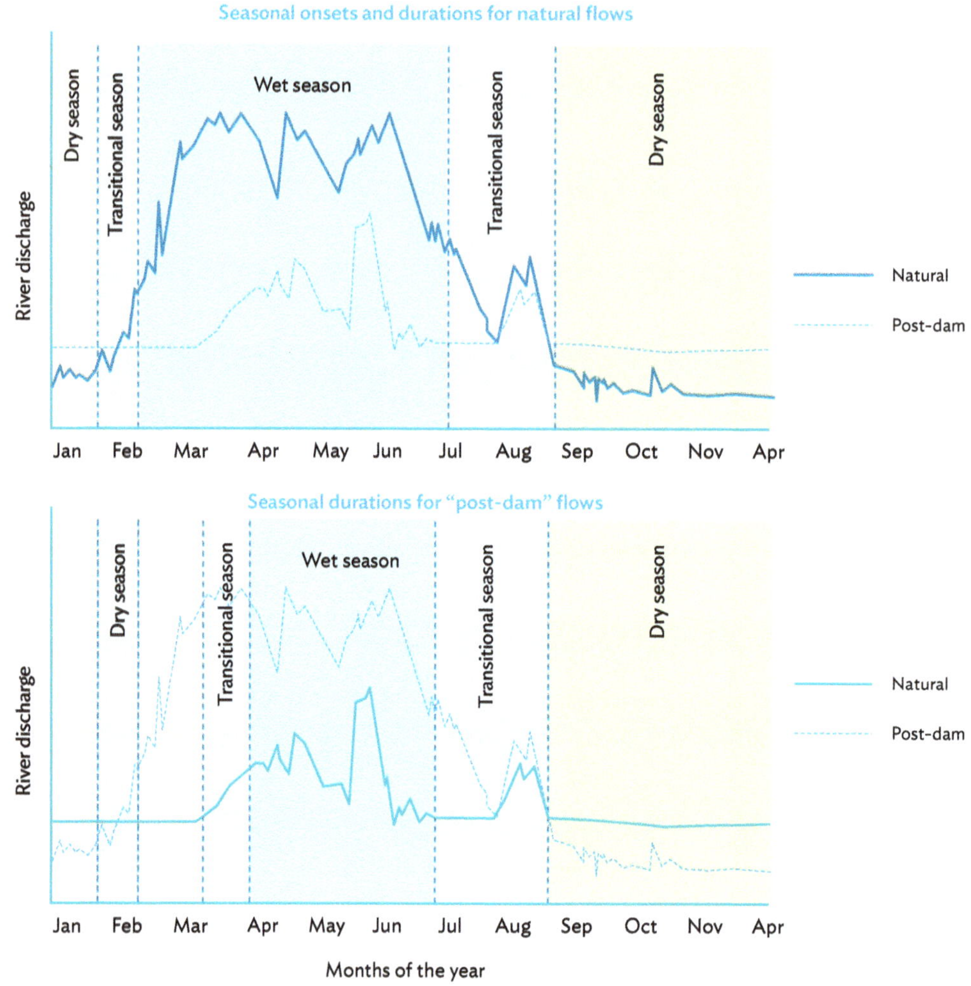

Top: Seasonal onsets and durations for natural flows.

Bottom: Seasonal durations for "post-dam" flows.

Source: Authors.

These changes can have important impacts on the ecosystem. For instance, many riverine animals—such as fish—breed in the wet season. During this period, they may need to migrate upstream and spawn; the eggs need time to develop, and once hatched, the fry need time to grow big enough to withstand the rigors of migrating downstream to the over-winter feeding grounds. A wet season that is only 2–3 months long may be too short for all these things to happen. Additionally, biological processes such as egg development in females are often linked to ambient cues other than discharge, e.g., temperature. In the post-dam example shown (Figure 1), there is a good chance that females are ready to spawn a full month before the river flows make it possible to migrate or spawn successfully. Reduced flood volumes also mean less flooding of riparian areas and floodplains, which are vital habitats for feeding and successful breeding for many species.

Dry season flows are critical, as this period is often the most challenging for plants and animals. Reducing flows or extending the duration of the dry season increases the stress on these species, prolonging the period of adverse conditions. Conversely, too much water in the dry season may mean that sections of the channel that should be dry remain wet, affecting the plants that can grow there, with knock-on effects on food availability and bank stability. Focusing solely on minimum flows can overlook other important changes, such as extended dry seasons, shortened or weakened wet seasons, mistimed onsets of seasonal flows, and reduced or poorly timed sediment delivery. These factors can significantly affect river health and may lead to incorrect conclusions about the river's expected condition. In some cases, small adjustments to release patterns that better align with natural seasonal timing can be more beneficial for river health than simply increasing minimum flows.

2.2 Sediment

Sediment transport is crucial for shaping river channels, maintaining habitats, and supporting primary production. Aquatic habitats depend on the balance of topography, water flow, sediment, and vegetation. Similarly, primary production—which forms the base of the food chain in rivers—relies on factors like shear stress, suspended solids, nutrients, temperature, and light penetration. Any changes in habitats or primary production affect the entire ecosystem.

River channels naturally adjust to changes in water flow or sediment processes, usually maintaining a state of balance in unregulated rivers due to the dynamic nature of natural flow patterns. Rivers are stable when their sediment load and sediment size match the river's flow and slope (Figure 2). If the sediment load or size decreases without a change in water flow, the riverbed and banks will erode. If water discharge increases without other changes, bed erosion is likely due to higher shear stress. Suspended sediment is also important for primary production, as it delivers nutrients, creates habitats, and affects light penetration, which is crucial for photosynthesis. Water resource projects—especially in-channel dams and reservoirs—often alter sediment loads and sizes downstream, causing changes in the river's shape and behavior.

By focusing solely on water flows, the potential impacts associated with erosion or deposition in downstream rivers may be overlooked, leading to erroneous conclusions regarding the expected river condition.

Figure 2: Lane's Balance, Showing the Interrelationship Between Sediment Loads, Median Sediment Size, Water Discharge, and Channel Slope

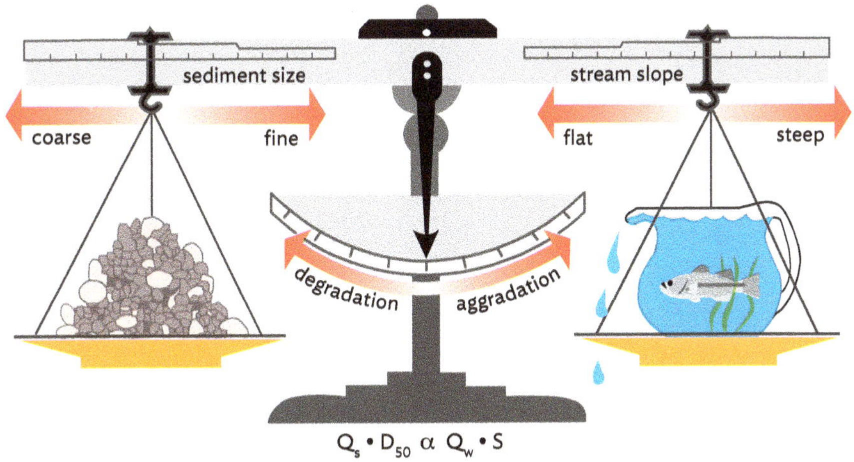

Source: E. Stein et al. 2014. Hydromodification Assessment and Management in California.

2.3 Water quality

Rivers transport dissolved materials from mountains to the sea, with the geology of the catchment area influencing river characteristics and ecosystems. Water quality, which includes factors like pH (a measure of acidity and alkalinity), temperature, oxygen levels, and conductivity, can change quickly with changes in flow. For example, rivers can become oxygen-depleted when dammed, harming aquatic life.

Dissolved substances—such as nutrients and metals—are essential for aquatic organisms but can be harmful in high concentrations. The timing of delivery is also important. Water quality can be further impacted by pathogens from industrial, municipal, or rural discharges, which may linger in the water or sediment.

River flows dilute and spread contaminants, so understanding the link between river flow and water quality is essential.

2.4 Connectivity

Connectivity is intimately linked with the impacts that barriers, natural or artificial, have on a river ecosystem. Migration upstream, downstream, and laterally is essential for the health of river ecosystems. While fish migration is the most well-known, many organisms—including plants, invertebrates, and crustaceans—rely on river connectivity to complete their life cycles. These movements support biodiversity as well as critical functions such as nutrient cycling and food supply.

Fish migrate for feeding, breeding, and/or thermal regulation, with journeys ranging from a few meters to hundreds of kilometers, triggered by seasonal patterns or environmental changes, such as river flows or temperature. Barriers to migration—such as dams without effective fish passage—are a major threat to freshwater biodiversity, disrupting migration routes, fragmenting populations, and undermining the reproductive and ecological integrity of species (Barbarossa et al. 2020). Focusing solely on water flows may overlook the ecological consequences of river fragmentation and disrupted connectivity.

2.5 Human Resource Use

In many parts of the world, the ecological condition of river ecosystems is declining because of multiple stressors, including pollution, overfishing, poaching, sediment mining, and land use changes like deforestation and urbanization. Each of these can independently harm river health, but their combined effects can be even more damaging, often exceeding the impact of river development alone. As a result, evaluating water-resource projects requires an ecosystem-based approach that accounts for all interacting components and activities from the projects as well as other ongoing pressures.

Neglecting to consider non-flow-related human impacts on river ecosystems results in inaccurate conclusions and—more importantly—missed opportunities to enhance ecosystem service delivery and safeguard river health.

3 Integration of Environmental Flows Assessments into the Project Cycle

3.1 ADB Projects Requiring an Environmental Flows Assessment

EFlows assessments are required for ADB-funded projects that will impact one or more of:

(i) **Hydrology:** Changes in flow magnitude, timing, or rate.

(ii) **Hydraulics:** Variations in water depth, width, current speed, or inundation extent.

(iii) **Sediment Supply:** Modifications in quality, volume, or timing of sediment delivery.

(iv) **Water Quality:** Alterations in dissolved or particulate matter, nutrients, heavy metals, pathogens, or temperature.

(v) **Biota Movement:** Disruption of the movement of organisms upstream, downstream, or into or out of tributaries and floodplains.

Dams and barrages are the most obvious developments affecting river ecosystems, but others can also disrupt river ecosystems directly (Table 1). Because a project's effects can extend far beyond the immediate area, upstream, downstream, and into connected ecosystems like floodplains, lakes, estuaries, and the ocean, projects should consider the potential for these impacts. Ignoring them can lead to unforeseen negative consequences and missed opportunities for maximizing benefits.

Table 1: Direct Impacts of ADB-Funded Developments on River Ecosystems

	Non-Flow-Related Impacts		Effects on Drivers of River Ecosystem Condition			
Type of Development	Habitat Destruction	Other Human Pressures	Hydrology	Sediment Supply	Water Quality	Migrations of Animals and Plants
Hydropower						
Water storage and supply						
Barrages						
Harbors and ferry ports						
Roads, bridges, embankments						
Wastewater management						
Drainage and flood control						
River transport						

Source: Prepared by Cate Brown, Lois Koehnken, and Francesco Ricciardi.

3.2 The Relationship Between Environmental Flows Assessments and Other ADB Assessment Types

Understanding the full environmental and social impacts of river projects requires an ecosystem-based approach: one that accounts for changes across time and space and considers potential mitigation measures. EFlows assessments provide a structured, process-based method for evaluating how developments influence river ecosystems and the services they provide.

EFlows assessments complement and strengthen a range of environmental and social assessment types used by ADB. These include:

(i) Environmental and social impact assessments (ESIAs), which focus on the impacts of individual projects.
(ii) Cumulative impact assessments (CIAs), which evaluate the collective effects of multiple developments within a river basin.

EFlows assessments add value by providing deeper insights into ecological cause-and-effect relationships. For example, once an ESIA has identified a species present in a river system, an EFlows assessment can determine how changes in flow regimes may affect that species and its habitat and make recommendations for mitigating these impacts through changes in project design and operation.

Given ADB's emphasis on project-level support, EFlows assessments are more frequently embedded within ESIAs. However, integrating basin-wide EFlows assessments into the early stages of planning—particularly within CIAs—is widely recognized as a more strategic approach for managing cumulative impacts. Despite institutional limitations that may constrain such integration, recent initiatives (e.g., Brown et al. 2020) show that several regional organizations have successfully developed basin-scale EFlows models in basins such as the Ganga, Mekong, Neelum-Jhelum, and Ravi. These efforts signal increasing recognition of EFlows assessments as a key tool for informed, integrated river basin planning.

Moreover, once developed, basin-wide EFlows models can be applied repeatedly—for evaluating individual projects, informing CIAs, or guiding basin-level development decisions—making them a valuable long-term planning resource.

3.2.1 Environmental and Social Impact Assessment

An ESIA is a standard tool for identifying, predicting, and evaluating the environmental and social effects of a proposed project. It also considers alternatives and aims to minimize adverse impacts while enhancing positive outcomes. ESIAs typically focus on individual projects and are often linked to national environmental permitting or approval processes (EIA Netherlands Commission).

EFlows assessments and ESIAs have clear areas of overlap and mutual support. For example:

(i) ESIAs document baseline environmental and social conditions, including species and habitat information.
(ii) EFlows assessments use this information to analyze how changes in river flows caused by a project could affect ecological processes and species survival.

Together, EFlows and ESIAs create a more comprehensive picture of project impacts, improving predictive accuracy and the design of mitigation strategies. For this reason, ADB often undertakes EFlows assessments alongside ESIAs, with each enhancing the effectiveness of the other (WBG 2018; Figure 3).

Figure 3: Recommended Alignment of Project Planning with an Environmental and Social Impact Assessment and Environmental Flows Assessment

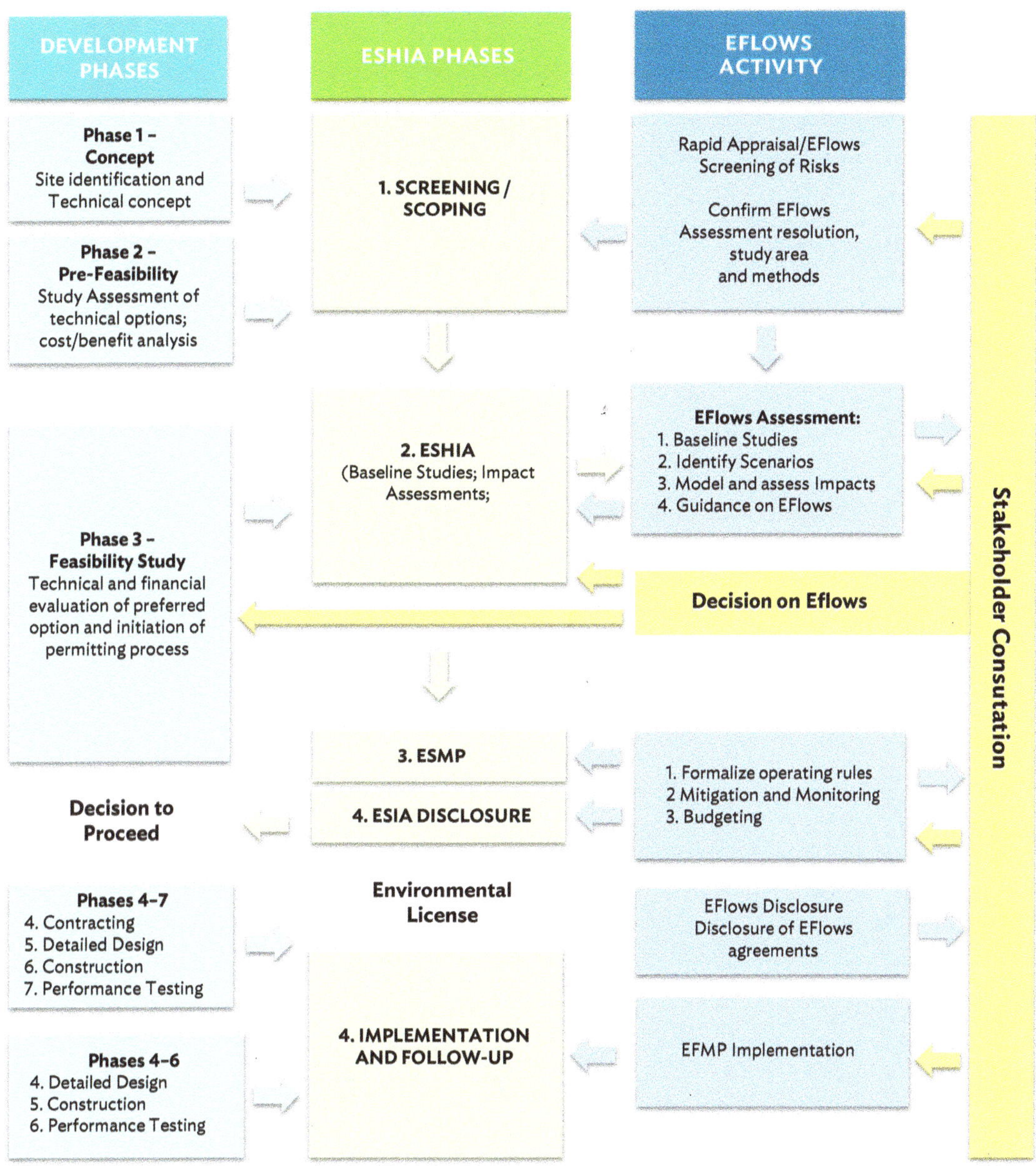

EFlows = environmental flows, EFMP = environmental flows management plan, ESHIA = environmental, social, and health impact assessment, ESIA = environmental and social impact assessment, ESMP = environmental and social management plan.

Source: After WBG. 2018. Good Practice Handbook: EFlows Assessments for hydropower projects.

3.2.2 Cumulative Impact Assessment

A CIA is a planning tool used to evaluate the combined effects of a proposed project together with those from other past, present, and reasonably foreseeable future developments within the same geographic and ecological context. This includes formally planned developments and unplanned, yet likely, activities triggered by the project that may arise over time or across different locations (International Finance Corporation [IFC] 2013; WBG 2016).

The six-step CIA process is structured to assess the impacts on valued ecosystem components, which are key environmental and social features prioritized for impact evaluation (IFC 2013). These may include

(i) physical features, habitats, and wildlife populations (e.g., biodiversity);
(ii) ecosystem services;
(iii) natural processes (e.g., water and nutrient cycles, microclimate);
(iv) social conditions (e.g., health, livelihoods); and/or
(v) cultural values (e.g., traditional practices and ceremonies).

As with ESIAs, effectively assessing cumulative impacts in river basins requires an ecosystem-based approach. This is especially true when addressing impacts on valued ecosystem components related to altered flow regimes, including changes in water, sediment, and biota movement. In this context, EFlows assessments are increasingly recognized as essential inputs to CIAs, helping to quantify the collective influence of multiple developments on riverine ecosystems.

Recent CIAs have incorporated detailed EFlows modeling to improve the quality and depth of assessment. Examples include studies in the Trishuli Basin (Nepal; IFC 2020), Karnali Basin (Nepal; EDF and GMR 2023), and the Lower Mekong Basin (Southeast Asia; Mekong River Commission 2017). These cases illustrate a growing trend toward integrating EFlows into basin-wide assessments, aligning with broader goals for sustainable water resource and development planning.

3.3 Contribution of Environmental Flows Assessments to ADB Safeguards

EFlows assessments provide essential data and insights that contribute to meeting the requirements of ADB's Environmental and Social Framework (ESF), particularly those related to ecosystem health, community well-being, and sustainable resource use. Their value lies in offering an integrated, ecosystem-based view of how projects affect river systems and the people who rely on them. Table 2 summarizes how information generated by an EFlows assessment can inform each safeguard.

Table 2: Contribution of Environmental Flows Assessments to ADB Safeguards

ESS No.	ESS Focus	EFlows Contribution
1	Environmental and Social Risk Management	Identifies impacts on water quality, aquatic ecosystems, migration pathways, invasive species, and public safety. Enhances stakeholder engagement and disclosure processes.
2	Labor and Working Conditions	No direct input from EFlows assessments.
3	Resource Conservation and Pollution Prevention	Provides information on water quality impacts and potential spread of invasive or pest species.
4	Health, Safety, and Security	Defines the river-related area of influence. Assesses risks to public health (e.g., disease vectors), dam-related safety, and ecosystem condition.
5	Land Acquisition and Land Use Restriction	Assesses impacts on river-dependent livelihoods and social well-being.
6	Biodiversity and Natural Resources Management	Evaluates impacts on aquatic habitats, species migration, biodiversity, and overall ecosystem health.
7	Indigenous Peoples	Highlights effects on traditional river-based practices such as fishing, farming, grazing, and material gathering.
8	Cultural Heritage	Assesses how changes in river flow affect culturally important river features, such as pools or reeds.
9	Climate Change	Identifies changes in river-related project risks and river conditions due to climate variability.
10	Stakeholder Engagement and Disclosure	Informs meaningful consultation through the identification of river-related risks and mitigation strategies.

Source: Asian Development Bank.

4 Key Features of an Effective Environmental Flows Assessment

EFlows assessments should provide clear information to governments and developers about the possible consequences of projects, along with options for mitigation through project location, design, and operation. They should also provide clear targets for post-implementation monitoring.

The assessments must be detailed enough to inform decisions about project development, design, and operation, ensuring that potential impacts on surface water ecosystems and the communities that depend on them are well understood. This aligns with a risk-based adaptive management approach, which is vital for sustainable development and addressing issues like poverty (WCD 2000; Hirji and Davis 2009).

The effectiveness of EFlows assessments is highly influenced by the methodologies employed, as historical legacy issues can affect their scope and reliability.

To effectively guide sustainable development, EFlows assessments should:

(i) Employ a flexible and adaptive framework to accommodate changing conditions and needs.

(ii) Integrate with other assessments (such as biodiversity and social impact assessments) to capture a holistic view of ecosystems and their uses.

(iii) Tailor assessments to specific ecosystem types (e.g., rivers, floodplains, estuaries) to ensure relevance.

(iv) Identify key drivers of ecosystem functioning, including hydrology, sediment transport, water quality, migration of animals, and social pressures.

(v) Characterize main ecosystem responders and feedback loops, considering habitats, species, and human activities.

(vi) Predict impacts of development, management practices, and climate change on ecosystems.

(vii) Provide accessible expert advice to assist stakeholders in making informed decisions about ecosystem health and services.

4.1 Scope of Assessment

4.1.1 Spatial

The spatial scale of an EFlows assessment depends on the intended purpose. For an individual proposed project, the study area should encompass the full extent of the expected influence of the project on the aquatic ecosystem. Depending on the intended nature, design, and operation of the project, this influence can extend upstream and downstream for many kilometers and, in some cases, laterally for many kilometers.

The issue of spatial scale can be challenging. EFlows are intended to address ecosystem health rather than the impacts of a single development, making the basin or sub-basin the most appropriate scale for assessment. However, project financing timelines often mean that a bank's involvement in a basin begins at the scale of an individual project. At a minimum, the study area for an EFlows assessment for an individual project should encompass:

(i) an extended river reach upstream of the development;
(ii) any river reach that is expected to be dewatered, e.g., between the dam wall and tailrace outlet in some hydropower plants; and
(iii) downstream of the development, to the extent that the impacts on the hydrology and sediment regime and migratory paths reach.

4.1.2 Temporal

EFlows assessments require long-term (preferably >30 years) hydrological and sediment time series datasets, where applicable, whether recorded, modeled, or estimated, against which ecosystem changes linked to changes in these can be assessed (United Nations Environment Programme [UNEP]-Nairobi Convention/Western Indian Ocean Marine Science Association 2020). This allows for consideration of seasonal trends and annual variations linked to drier and wetter periods, and/or climate change.

4.2 Methods

Published EFlows assessment methods vary in complexity from simple hydrological indices aimed at setting minimum dry season discharges to comprehensive ecosocial models that explore the interconnections within river ecosystems and their relationship with human communities. Only a few of the published methods have been applied regularly, and many of the earlier methods ignore ecosystem functioning, do not reflect true ecosystem health, and fail to engage stakeholders.

The aspects of the river that are typically categorized as EFlows include the quantity, timing, and quality of the flows of water, sediment, and biota. Technically included within this definition are the impacts of barriers to dispersal and migration of biota, sediment and nutrient trapping, downstream impacts of hydropeaking, water temperature of spills from the dam, and the flushing of sediments. However, these aspects of EFlows are often overlooked. The level of EFlows in their entirety, in part, determines the level at which freshwater and estuarine ecosystems are sustained and the level of ecosystem services that they provide.

There are five main categories of EFlows assessment methods (Tharme et al. 2003):

(i) Hydrological Assessments. Focus on minimum flow recommendations, assessing only the quantity of water available in rivers.
(ii) Hydraulic Assessments. Consider hydrology and the relationships between hydraulics and habitat availability. Some more modern hydraulic methods also consider sediments, recognizing the physical processes that shape river ecosystems.
(iii) Habitat Modeling. Mostly used for low flows (dry season) based on the empirical relationship between environmental variables such as depth and velocity, and usable habitat for selected target species, life stages, or aquatic communities. More recent iterations use sophisticated models based on fuzzy logic (e.g., Marsili-Libelli et al. 2013).

(iv) Holistic Assessments. Encompass numerous components of riverine and estuarine ecosystems, integrating ecosystem services and social values into evaluations of river health and function.

(v) Ecosocial Modeling. Incorporates aspects of the above approaches and utilizes decision-support systems to provide interactive and scenario-based assessments that consider multiple ecological and social factors and their interactions across river reaches, sub-basins, and whole basins.

Most EFlows assessment methods depend, to varying degrees, on expert judgment and peer-reviewed scientific literature. Several methods have also been specifically designed for data-limited settings, making them broadly adaptable for use across different projects.

The method chosen for an EFlows assessment significantly influences the level of detail and overall utility of the findings. While rapid, generic assessments may seem cost-effective or expedient, they often overlook key ecological and social dynamics, leading to misguided decisions, increased project risks, and long-term environmental or community impacts (King and Brown 2018a). Conversely, well-designed, in-depth assessments contribute to more informed planning, enhance respect for ecological and social systems, and foster sustainable outcomes for river ecosystems and the communities that depend on them.

Table 3 outlines a range of EFlows assessment methods. It categorizes each method by assessment type, ecosystem applicability, resolution, methodological approach (prescriptive or scenario-based), key variables considered, and examples of use. Methods based on outdated or unscientific assumptions—such as the widely misused 10% flow rule—are discouraged and therefore excluded from this table, despite their continued application in some contexts.

Table 3: Examples of Environmental Flows Assessment Methods, Scope, Resolution, and Applications in ADB Projects

Method	Resolution	Type of Ecosystems	Format	Potential Consideration of:							Previous Use in ADB Projects
				Hydrology	Hydraulics	Water Quality	Geomorphology	Ecology	Other Pressures[a]	Social Uses	
Hydrological											
Tennant	Low[b]	River	Prescriptive[c]								Brenwe HPP (Appendix A)
Hydraulic											
Wetted perimeter (Gippel and Stewardson)	Low	River	Prescriptive								–
Habitat modeling											
PHABSIM (Jowett et al.)	Medium/ High	River	Prescriptive	Low flows							–
CASIMIR (Marsili-Libelli et al.)	Medium	River	Scenario[d]								Unknown
Holistic											
BBM (King and Louw)	Medium/ High	River and wetland	Prescriptive								Unknown
Ecosocial modeling											
DRIFT (Joubert)	Medium/ High	River (e.g., Brown et al.) Floodplain (e.g., GIZ) Estuary (e.g., GWP)	Scenario								Gulpur HPP (high resolution; Appendix A)

ADB = Asian Development Bank, BBM = building block methodology, CASIMIR = Computer Aided Simulation Model for Instream Flow and Riparia, DRIFT = downstream response to imposed flow transformations, GIZ = Deutsche Gesellschaft für Internationale Zusammenarbeit, HPP = hydroelectric power project, PHABSIM = Physical Habitat Simulation System.

[a] Other pressures include consideration of improved management of existing natural resource use, such as mining and fishing, where applicable, e.g., Gulpur HPP (section B.1.2).

[b] Low-resolution desktop techniques based on indices derived from more detailed studies.

[c] Prescriptive methods: Recommend minimum flows to achieve specific objectives (World Bank Group. 2018. Good Practice Handbook: EFlows Assessments for hydropower projects).

[d] Scenario-based methods: Focus on the relationships between changes in the river flow and a range of aspects of the river and provide predicted ecological (and social) outcomes for a range of scenarios. The decision on EFlows lies with ADB, the borrowers/clients, and stakeholders, as appropriate.

Sources: C. Brown et al. 2017. Achieving an environmentally sustainable outcome for the Gulpur hydropower project in the Poonch River Mahaseer National Park, Pakistan. *Sustainable Water Resources Management*. 5. pp. 611–628; C. J. Gippel and M. J. Stewardson, 1998. Use of wetted perimeter in defining minimum environmental flows. *Regulated Rivers: Research and Management*. 14(1). pp. 53–67; Global Water Partnership (GWP). 2023. Services for an integrated Flows assessment to facilitate the development and agreement of "Objective EFlows" at key sites in the Pungwe Basin. EFlows Scenario Assessment Report; I. Jowett, J. Hayes, and M. Duncan. 2008. A guide to instream habitat survey methods and analysis. NIWA; J. King and D. Louw. 1998. Instream flow assessments for regulated rivers in South Africa using the Building Block Methodology. *Aquatic Ecosystem Health and Management*. 1. pp. 109–124, S. Marsili-Libelli, E. Giusti, and A. Nocita. 2013. A new instream flow assessment method based on fuzzy habitat suitability and large scale river modelling. *Environmental Modelling and Software*. 41. pp. 27–38; D. L. Tennant. 1976. Instream flow regimens for fish, wildlife, recreation and related environmental resources. *Fisheries*. 1(4). pp. 6–10; Wildlands. 2021. Preliminary aquatic ecology assessment for the Brenwe Hydropower Project, Malekula, Vanuatu: aquatic habitats and species.

EFlows assessments should be transparent and scientifically rigorous. They must clearly justify the chosen methods, identify underlying assumptions, and reference relevant literature. Scenario-based approaches align well with ADB's risk-based adaptive management framework (ADB 2024). These methods evaluate a range of possible outcomes rather than prescribe a single "correct" flow regime. By simulating multiple flow scenarios and exploring associated ecological and social risks, they provide stakeholders with the information needed to make informed, context-specific decisions.

In contrast, prescriptive methods offer fixed recommendations (e.g., a high-flow release to "flush debris and maintain habitats") without fully explaining the consequences of not achieving these flows (e.g., infilled pools and embedded riffle areas). This failure to describe the physical and biological consequences of not achieving the recommended EFlows limits their value in decision-making processes that require a broad understanding of trade-offs and uncertainties (Brown et al. 2020; King and Brown 2018b).

Ultimately, scenario-based assessments empower stakeholders by illustrating the potential consequences of various management choices and enabling collaborative, evidence-based decision-making. Unlike prescriptive methods, scenario-based approaches do not produce a single "recommended" EFlows value. Instead, they describe the expected ecological and social responses to different combinations of design parameters, operating rules, or management approaches. This enables stakeholders to evaluate trade-offs and select the most appropriate course of action based on their priorities, values, and objectives. Once a particular scenario is selected, the driving parameters encompassed in that scenario (hydrology, sediment, and biotic migration) are used to set the EFlows for the project.

4.2.1 Resolution

Generally, low-resolution methods use different approaches compared to medium- and high-resolution methods. While medium- and high-resolution EFlows assessments often follow a similar overall methodology, they differ in the level of detail. High-resolution methods incorporate more specific data, such as species survival, sediment reduction, and the effects of peaking-power releases, making them better suited for meeting the unique needs of individual projects. Medium- and high-resolution methods examine the relationship between changes in river flow and various ecosystem components, with high-resolution assessments covering more aspects of the ecosystem and requiring more extensive data collection. Furthermore, both approaches often include models to assess the potential impacts on local communities, agriculture, navigation, and cultural environments (WBG 2018).

Regardless of the resolution level, every EFlows assessment must, at a minimum, evaluate how changes in river hydrology, such as volume, timing, magnitude, and duration, will affect the river ecosystem and the people who depend on it. In addition, other factors that could impact river ecology should also be considered, regardless of the resolution used.

These factors include:

(i) changes in the amount, type, and timing of sediment reaching different parts of the river;
(ii) changes in the chemistry of the water reaching different parts of the river;
(iii) changes in river connectivity, such as fish migration or movement between the river and floodplain; and
(iv) changes in human uses of the river, such as fishing, sediment mining, and other activities.

Since low-resolution methods cannot effectively integrate these factors into the EFlows assessment, and because these analyses often require input from specialists across various disciplines, it is advisable to use a medium- or high-resolution approach if these factors are likely to significantly influence the assessment.

4.3 Factors Influencing the Recommended Resolution of an Environmental Flows Assessment

Requiring a single method for EFlows assessments can limit innovation. However, establishing standard criteria for determining the appropriate level of resolution and minimum output formats can be beneficial. Ideally, the level of assessment should be defined before issuing requests for project proposals, as it influences team composition, budget, and study duration. EFlows practitioners can adapt methods to specific circumstances, so assumptions about cost, suitability, or resolution may not always hold.

More detailed EFlows assessments provide a more comprehensive prediction of project impacts, reducing unintended consequences and allowing stakeholders to contribute to planning and management. To ensure the selection process is rigorous, the chosen method should be justified, demonstrate suitability, state underlying assumptions, and reference published literature.

The resolution of an assessment should be influenced by several factors, including

(i) project location, design, and operation;
(ii) spatial context;
(iii) biodiversity and river use; and
(iv) magnitude of expected impacts on water, sediment, and biota flows.

The decision-making flowchart in Figure 4 supports consistent selection of EFlows assessment resolution based on project features and ecological sensitivity. Starting in the top left-hand corner, the flowchart poses a series of questions that, once answered, will lead to a recommended resolution for the EFlows assessment.

Figure 4: Flowchart for Determining the Resolution of an Environmental Flows Assessment

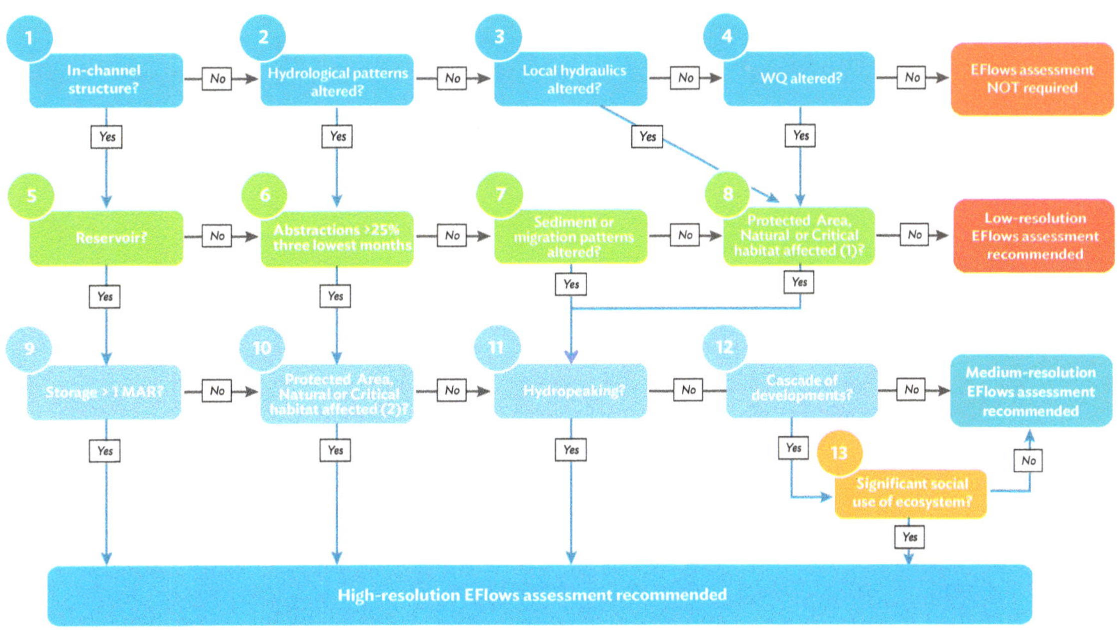

Eflows = environmental flows, MAR = mean annual runoff, WQ = water quality.
Source: Authors.

4.3.1 Question (Q) 1: Physical In-Channel Barrier?

Projects that create physical in-channel barriers—such as weirs, dams, or barrages—are more likely to affect river flows than projects that do not create physical barriers, such as bridges, roads, or river transport projects.

(i) If a project will create a physical in-channel barrier, the answer is YES, the next question is whether there is a reservoir associated with the barrier (Q5; section 4.3.5).

(ii) If the answer is NO, the next question is whether the water, sediment, or migration patterns of biota are expected to be altered by the project (Q2; section 4.3.2)

4.3.2 Q2: Hydrological Patterns Altered?

Projects altering water, sediment, or biota flow patterns can significantly impact river ecosystems, even without in-channel structures. Examples include sewage and other effluent outfalls that could create water quality barriers to migration, run-of-river abstractions that could reduce flows and change seasonal timing of flows, dredging that could disrupt sediment patterns and water quality, and noise from river traffic can inhibit the migration of dolphins.

(i) If the project is likely to alter the volume or timing of water or sediment, or affect the timing and success of animal or plant migrations, the answer is YES, the next question is whether abstraction levels are likely to exceed 25% of the natural dry season discharge (Q6; section 4.3.6).

(ii) If the answer is NO, the next question is whether the project is likely to alter local hydraulic characteristics (Q3; section 4.3.3).

4.3.3 Q3: Altered Local Hydraulics?

In-channel structures that do not create barriers can still affect the speed, depth, or direction of river flows, which can affect deposition or erosion of sediments and the availability of habitats. Examples include bridge pylons, boat-taxi harbors, and riverbank stabilization projects. For example, bridge pylons in the Brahmaputra River created deep pools that attracted fishers and dolphins, leading to unintended dolphin fatalities.

This question requires an appraisal of the proposed project in terms of its potential effects on ecohydraulics.[1]

(i) If the answer is YES, the next question is whether the project is in, or is likely to affect, a protected area or critical habitat (Q8; section 4.3.8).

(ii) If the answer is NO, the next question is whether the project is likely to alter localized water quality characteristics (Q4; section 4.3.4).

4.3.4 Q4: Water Quality Changes?

Discharges to rivers, e.g., sewage or industrial effluents, have the potential to significantly affect ecosystem functioning through numerous avenues, including toxic effects, but also changes in temperature, nutrient delivery and/or light penetration, which affect primary production and change aquatic life.

(i) If a project is likely to alter the water quality of a river, the answer is YES, and the next question is whether the project is in, or is likely to affect, a protected area or critical habitat (section Q8; 4.3.8).

(ii) If the answer is NO: **No EFlows Assessment required.**

1 Ecohydraulics: The interaction between water flow patterns and physical river features, and how these influence sediment movement, erosion, deposition, and aquatic habitat availability.

4.3.5 Q5: Reservoir?

Reservoirs created by in-channel dams can drastically change river flow regimes, impacting water levels, sediment transport, and migration pathways.

(i) If the project will create a reservoir, regardless of its size, then the answer is YES, and the next question is whether the volume of the reservoir is greater than the volume of the mean annual runoff (MAR) flowing down the river (Q9; section 4.3.9).

(ii) If the answer is NO, the next question is whether the project is associated with water abstractions that exceed 25% of the natural dry season discharge (Q6; section 4.3.6).

4.3.6 Q6: Abstractions >25% of Natural Dry Season Discharge?[2]

Abstractions that exceed 25% of the river's natural median dry-season discharge can significantly impact river ecosystems by altering seasonal flow patterns and sediment movement.

(i) If the project will result in abstractions of water from the river that are >25% of the river's natural dry-season discharge, then the answer is YES, and the next question is whether the project is likely to alter the volume or timing of water or sediment (Q7: section 4.3.7).

(ii) If the answer is NO, the next question is whether the project is in, or is likely to affect, a protected area or Critical Habitat (Q8; section 4.3.8).

4.3.7 Q7: Altered Sediment or Migration Patterns?

(i) If the project is likely to alter the volume or timing of water or sediment, or affect the timing and success of animal or plant migrations, the answer is YES, and the next question is whether these alterations are a result of hydropeaking (Q11: section 4.3.11).

(ii) If the answer is NO, the next question is whether the project is in, or is likely to affect, a protected area or natural or critical habitat (Q8; section 4.3.8).

4.3.8 Q8: Protected Areas, Natural, or Critical Habitats (1)?

Projects affecting protected, natural, or critical habitats must assess their impacts on biodiversity and comply with ADB safeguards, ensuring that no significant degradation of natural habitats or endangerment of species occurs. For projects with an in-channel barrier and a reservoir, this requires at least a medium-resolution EFlows assessment. Natural habitats are areas composed of assemblages of plant and animal species of largely native origin, where human activity has not substantially modified an area's primary ecological function or species composition. Critical habitats are a subset of natural and modified habitats, comprising areas of highest biodiversity value of significant importance to one or more types of priority biodiversity features. This includes areas of very high biodiversity conservation value and of significant importance to one or more types of priority biodiversity features, including (i) threatened ecosystems, (ii) geographically restricted ecosystems, (iii) threatened species, (iv) endemic and geographically-restricted species, (v) geographically restricted assemblages, (vi) aggregations of migratory or congregatory species, (vii) areas associated with key evolutionary processes, or (viii) ecological functions that are vital to maintaining the viability of priority biodiversity features (ADB 2024).

[2] Natural dry season discharge: The median flow of water in a river or stream during the naturally occurring dry season, without the influence of human alterations such as dams, diversions, or extractions. It is typically expressed in cubic meters per second (m^3/s) and calculated from long-term hydrological records to capture typical seasonal low-flow conditions.

(i) If the answer is YES, the project is in a protected area or natural habitat or critical habitat, then the next question reverts to whether the project will involve hydropeaking (Q11; section 4.3.11).

(ii) If the answer is NO: **Low-Resolution EFlows Assessment is recommended.**

4.3.9 Q9: Storage >100% of Mean Annual Runoff?[3]

Dams with reservoir storage greater than the river's MAR can significantly impact downstream flow regimes, including the onset and duration of seasons, seasonal variability, flood attenuation, sediment supply, and migration patterns.

(i) If the project can store a volume of water that is greater than the MAR of the river on which it is situated, then the answer is YES: **High-resolution EFlows assessment is recommended.**

(ii) If the answer is NO, then the next question is whether the project is in, or is likely to affect, a protected area or natural or critical habitat (Q10; section 4.3.10).

4.3.10 Q10: Protected Areas, Natural or Critical Habitats (2)?

See section 4.3.8 for definitions.

(i) If the answer is YES, then: **High-resolution E-Flow assessment is recommended.**

(ii) If the answer is NO, then the next question is whether the project will involve hydropeaking (Q11; section 4.3.11).

4.3.11 Q11: Hydropeaking

Hydropeaking, or rapid daily flow fluctuations, can cause numerous ecological issues, such as habitat fragmentation, erosion, and altered species communities. The timing and magnitude of fluctuations are critical to understanding their impact.

(i) If hydropeaking is planned, then the answer is YES: **High-resolution EFlows assessment is recommended.**

(ii) If the answer is NO, the next question is if the project is in a cascade of developments (Q12; section 4.3.12).

4.3.12 Q12: Cascade of Developments

The location of a proposed project relative to existing developments can influence its potential impacts, with prior developments possibly reducing the sensitivity of the river to new disturbances.

(i) If the answer is YES, the next question is whether there is significant social use of the ecosystem, e.g., fishing, sediment mining, or boating (Q13; section 4.3.13).

(ii) If the answer is NO: **Medium-resolution EFlows assessment is recommended.**

3 Mean annual runoff (MAR): The average total volume of water discharged from a catchment or river basin over a year, calculated over a multi-year period (often 20–30 years) to account for natural variability. It is usually expressed in cubic meters per year (m^3/year) or in terms of average flow rate in cubic meters per second (m^3/s).

4.3.13 Q13: Significant Social Use

Social use of a river affects its ecosystem and the resolution of the EFlows assessment. Projects may impact fisheries, sediment mining, or other community uses of the river, which should be considered in the assessment.

(i) If many people use the river for many activities, or if there is one or more activities considered important to the downstream stakeholders, then the answer is YES: **High-resolution EFlows assessment is recommended.**

(ii) If the answer is NO: Medium-resolution EFlows assessment is recommended.

4.4 Dealing with Data Limitations

Data paucity is a common challenge in river systems across many ADB developing member countries, driven by factors such as:

(i) the remote location of rivers, which complicates long-term hydrological monitoring;

(ii) limited availability of long-term rainfall and river flow data, particularly in small island developing states; and/or

(iii) institutional and capacity constraints in fragile and conflict-affected situations, which impede effective water-resource monitoring.

While these data limitations are real, they should not preclude the application of EFlows principles. EFlows are essential to sustaining freshwater ecosystems, supporting community livelihoods, managing sediment transport, and enabling the movement of migratory species. In developing member regions where communities are highly dependent on natural resources, careful integration of EFlows into project planning is environmentally responsible and critical for achieving long-term development outcomes.

Although earlier guidance sometimes suggested that data-poor contexts justify simplified EFlows assessments, growing experience shows the opposite: data-scarce environments often demand more robust, adaptive, and context-specific approaches to effectively uphold EFlows principles. Project teams must therefore plan for flexibility in assessment methodologies and engage early with local stakeholders and knowledge systems to address data gaps. There is no one-size-fits-all approach. The priority should be to proceed with caution, using the best available evidence. This approach helps ensure that project investments remain environmentally sustainable and socially inclusive, even when conventional datasets are lacking.

Many EFlows methods are specifically designed to work with limited data, enabling assessments to proceed. Experienced EFlows practitioners should be able to suggest an approach that meets project requirements within regional contexts. However, for rivers where available data are particularly sparse or non-existent, it is essential that the terms of reference (TORs) (Appendix B: Generic Templates for Terms of Reference) clearly state:

(i) the location;

(ii) which kinds of data are limited, and why;

(iii) limitations, if any, on primary data collection;

(iv) the required level of assessment (based on Figure 4);

(v) the importance of basing the assessment on one or more of the following:

  (a) global datasets;

  (b) proportional change;

(c) pragmatic, comparative approach;

(d) social science and local knowledge; and/or

(e) other sources of information, provided clearly motivated.

4.4.1 Global Datasets

There is an increasing number of global datasets available for developing hydrological time series and other data relevant to EFlows assessments. The most routinely used among these are:

(i) Climate Hazards Group InfraRed Precipitation with Station data. High-resolution precipitation data useful for rainfall-runoff hydrological modeling in areas where snowfall is not a major component of precipitation.

(ii) Global Runoff Data Centre. Provides observed river discharge data from thousands of stations worldwide. These data are valuable for calibrating rainfall-runoff models, disaggregating monthly discharges into daily discharges, or serving as proxy data.

(iii) HydroSHEDS. High-resolution river network and watershed data derived from NASA's Shuttle Radar Topography Mission elevation data. These datasets are freely available in standard geographic information system (GIS) formats and provide the geospatial framework for a wide range of assessments, including hydrological, environmental, conservation, socioeconomic, and human health applications.

4.4.2 Proportional Change

In the absence of data, EFlows assessments can be undertaken using proportional changes in hydrology, sediment supply, and/or barriers to migration. For instance, the percentage increase or decrease from the baseline in the following variables:

(i) dry season low flows;

(ii) wet season low flows;

(iii) onset of dry or wet season;

(iv) duration of dry, wet, or transitional seasons;

(v) magnitude of flood events;

(vi) sediment supply in dry, wet, or transitional seasons; and/or

(vii) successful migration upstream and downstream.

Information to construct these proportional changes can be obtained from project design, discussions with the developer, literature on similar projects or rivers, or remote sensing, such as floodplain areas.

4.4.3 Pragmatic, Comparative Approach

EFlows assessments should characterize

(i) the river system in question, considering its geomorphological zone, its flow regime, ecological features, and seasonal dynamics; and

(ii) the design, location, and proposed operating rules of the proposed project.

Based on this, a comparable river–project combination can be identified where EFlows have been studied or implemented at the recommended level of detail. Drawing on observed or predicted relationships from these analogous systems can provide a realistic and context-sensitive basis for estimating likely EFlows under different development scenarios (e.g., Bukhari et al. 2025).

4.4.4 Social Science and Local Knowledge

In data-poor settings, local and traditional knowledge are essential complements to scientific data. People living near rivers—such as farmers, clothing washers, and fishers—often have a detailed understanding of river behavior, uses, seasonal patterns, and cultural importance. Incorporating this knowledge into EFlows assessments can improve accuracy, capture cultural dimensions, and promote local engagement in decision-making (Vos 2020).

4.5 Staffing for environmental flows assessments

The consultant(s) must have the qualifications, skills, and experience required to conduct an EFlows assessment. Consulting firms should have a strong track record in EFlows work and successful project delivery. If these capabilities are lacking in-house, they should partner with firms that possess them.

The team leader must be an experienced EFlows practitioner, responsible for managing the entire assessment. This includes advising stakeholders, coordinating the team, securing and managing data, selecting scenarios, and ensuring quality assurance. The role also covers financial management, team leadership, capacity building, stakeholder engagement, and report preparation. The team leader should have a clear understanding of how development projects can affect ecosystem functions, be familiar with suitable EFlows assessment methods, and be skilled in leading multidisciplinary teams.

The consultant's team must include, at a minimum, the positions listed in Table 4. One qualified individual may take on more than one role. The team composition can vary across work streams, but all members must hold relevant professional qualifications from recognized institutions and, ideally, have prior experience in physical and cultural settings like the project area.

Templates for TORs for EFlows assessment of different resolutions are provided in Appendix B: Generic Templates for Terms of Reference.

4.6 Assessment Process

A typical EFlows assessment process should comprise the following main steps:

1. Inception phase
2. Scenario selection
3. Collation and/or modeling of input data
4. Field data collection
5. Specialist studies and setup of assessment framework
6. EFlows assessment and reporting
7. Stakeholder consultation and expert review
8. Decision on EFlows and setting targets
9. Preparation of EFlows Management Plan
10. Monitoring
11. Adaptive management and revision.

Table 4: Guidance on Team Composition for Different Environmental Flows Assessment Resolution Levels

Role	Team member	Experience	EFlows assessment resolution		
			High	Medium	Low
Team Lead	EFlows practitioner	>10 years of experience in assessing EFlows on similar ecosystems			
Discipline specialists	Hydrologist	>5 years of experience			
	Hydraulician	>5 years of experience, including demonstrable track record of ecohydraulic modeling for EFlows assessments			
	Water quality specialist	>5 years of experience in similar ecosystems			
	Geomorphologist/sedimentologist	>5 years of experience in similar ecosystems			
	Botanist	>5 years of experience and an in-depth knowledge of the plant communities in similar ecosystems			
	Macroinvertebrate ecologist	>5 years of experience and an in-depth knowledge of the macroinvertebrates in similar ecosystems			
	Fish ecologist	>5 years of experience and an in-depth knowledge of the fish communities in similar ecosystems			
	Social specialist	>5 years of experience and an in-depth knowledge of the river uses and customs in the study area			
Technical	GIS technician	>2 years of experience			

Eflows = environmental flows, GIS = geographic information system.
Source: Authors.

The parties with the main responsibility for each of these steps are outlined in Table 5.

Table 5: Parties Responsible for Each Step in an Environmental Flows Assessment

Step	Responsible Party
Inception phase	Consultant
Scenario selection	Consultant, developer, and ADB
Collation and/or modeling of input data	Consultant and developer
Field data collection	Consultant
Specialist studies and setup of assessment framework	Consultant
Environmental flows assessment and reporting	Consultant
Stakeholder consultation and expert review	Developer and ADB
Decision on environmental flows and setting targets	Developer and ADB
Environmental flows management plan	Consultant, developer, and ADB
Monitoring	Developer/operator
Adaptive management and revision	Developer/operator

ADB = Asian Development Bank.
Source: Authors.

4.6.1 Inception Phase

The inception phase should start with a thorough review of the project's design and how it will operate. This review includes examining project plans, reports, research, and related literature. It is also important to consider the project within the context of the wider river catchment—including its potential interactions with other existing or planned projects in the area—which may either amplify or reduce overall impacts. This review will help assess how the project might change water and sediment flows—in timing and amount—and how far downstream these changes will be felt. Key concerns include effects on fish migration and breeding areas, other river and stream ecosystems, public safety, water use, and cultural sites.

The findings from this phase will help finalize

(i) what aquatic ecosystems should be included or excluded,
(ii) what ecosystem services the water system provides,
(iii) what environmental indicators might be affected,
(iv) what existing data or models can be used,
(v) the boundaries of the study area,
(vi) where and how many EFlows assessment sites are needed,
(vii) the assessment approach and methods,
(viii) the project team,
(ix) whether more field data are needed, and
(x) early ideas for different design and operation scenarios to be evaluated.

Project design refers to elements such as dam height, reservoir capacity, and in-stream structures, including any planned fish passages. Project operation covers how water is released, how sediment is managed, and the resulting conditions in the river downstream.

TIP:
Check whether other EFlows work has been done in the region or basin. EFlows models set up for one part of a basin can be extrapolated to others at a fraction of the time and cost of starting from scratch.

4.6.2 Scenario selection

Scenario analysis helps explore future options by illustrating the potential benefits and costs of each. This approach supports governments, developers, and other stakeholders in identifying an appropriate balance between resource protection and development. The selection of scenarios should be led by stakeholders, with guidance and technical support from the EFlows team. The different scenarios may include current or proposed operating rules for infrastructure, species protection targets, natural resource management, water quality measures, and/or climate change forecasts. Once selected, the scenarios are then modeled for consideration in the EFlows assessment.

4.6.3 Scenario-generation modeling

Scenario-based EFlows methods use modeled operational rules tailored to the specific project under evaluation. For each scenario, these rules—covering factors such as the timing and volume of water and sediment releases downstream—are adjusted. Models reflecting the project design and the chosen scenario then generate time series data of these releases, which form the basis for assessment. Examples include the Scenario Generation Model (SGM; HBP 2023), which was specifically developed for computing long-term (>30-year) time series of power generation and turbine flows for use in EFlows assessments.

4.6.4 Collation and/or modeling of input data

The types of datasets required depend on the EFlows assessment method (Table 6).

There is a combination of tools and models that support EFlows assessments. Application of these tools tends to be project- and basin-specific, depending on the availability of data, the level of EFlows assessment being undertaken, and the characteristics of the affected river ecosystem. Examples of routinely used models include rainfall-runoff, scenario-generation, ecohydraulic, or hydrodynamic models. Others, such as water-resource, sediment, water quality, and/or fisheries models, have also been used in some assessments (section 4.6.3).

4.6.4.1 Hydrology

A daily time series of hydrological data, preferably for the natural and the baseline states (if these differ), is essential for all EFlows assessments. Monthly hydrological data are not recommended for use, as they provide limited insight into how water is distributed throughout each month; and an understanding of the daily, seasonal, and annual variations in the flow of water is crucial to understanding a river's response to change. Typically, the hydrological time series are collected from gauge stations in the study river.

If measured hydrological data are not available, then the time series can be modeled (section 4.6.4.1.1). In general, the data used for EFlows assessments should match those used in the design of any proposed projects.

Table 6: Types of Datasets Required for Different Environmental Flows Assessment Methods

<table>
<tr><th>Method (Table 3)</th><th>Daily Hydrological Time Series</th><th>Hydraulics</th><th>Sediments</th><th>Water Quality</th><th>Connectivity</th></tr>
<tr><td>Tennant</td><td rowspan="6">Essential</td><td>Not used</td><td rowspan="3" colspan="4">Not used</td></tr>
<tr><td>Wetted perimeter</td><td rowspan="2">Essential</td></tr>
<tr><td>IFIM</td></tr>
<tr><td>CASIMIR</td><td rowspan="3" colspan="2">Recommended
Recommended</td><td>Not used</td><td>Not used</td></tr>
<tr><td>BBM</td><td>Not used</td><td></td></tr>
<tr><td>DRIFT</td><td>Recommended</td><td></td></tr>
</table>

BBM = building block methodology, CASIMIR = Computer Aided Simulation Model for Instream Flow and Riparia, DRIFT = downstream response to imposed flow transformations, IFIM = Instream Flow Incremental Methodology.

Source: Authors.

4.6.4.1.1 Rainfall-runoff modeling

Hydrological modeling simulates the conversion of precipitation into runoff within a watershed, using mathematical models to analyze and predict water flow and availability. It is particularly useful in regions where reliable hydrological data are unavailable. Another key application is incorporating predicted climate change impacts into river hydrology, which in turn informs EFlows assessments. Many models, however, are limited to delivering monthly volume estimates based on rainfall or snowfall, adjusted for the watershed's climatic, geological, and morphological characteristics. As a result, the output from these models typically needs to be disaggregated into daily flows using measured records. In contrast, more advanced models can simulate daily river discharge. The choice between these approaches depends on site-specific factors, as both have their limitations (John et al. 2021). An experienced hydrologist, in liaison with the EFlows practitioner, should be able to explain the differences between the models and their relevance to the project's application.

4.6.4.2 Hydraulics

Basic ecohydraulic modeling is desirable in most cases to convert river discharge (m^3/s) into more ecologically meaningful parameters, such as depth (meters - m), wetted area (square meters - m^2), velocity (meters per second - m/s), and shear stress (Pascals - Pa).[4]

For hydraulically complex ecosystems—such as floodplains and wetlands—hydrodynamic modeling is required, as hydrology alone cannot provide essential information on the timing, depth, extent, and duration of inundation. Hydrodynamic modeling is also required for

(i) routing flows downstream where hydropower plants are planning on hydropeaking; and

(ii) estuaries, which have the complications of channel morphology, bidirectional movement of water (river and sea), tidal influences, and resultant salinity profiles.

[4] Shear stress: The force per unit area exerted by flowing water parallel to the riverbed or channel surface, which influences sediment movement, erosion, and habitat conditions.

4.6.4.2 Sediments

If a project is expected to impact sediment flow in a river, having access to daily or monthly time series data on suspended sediment loads and grain size distributions is essential. Ideally, these datasets should represent the natural conditions of the river and the baseline conditions at the time of the study. Such data are highly valuable for EFlows assessments. In many cases, these data are already collected as part of project design and monitoring requirements.

When such time series are unavailable, potential impacts on sediment transport can still be estimated. While not ideal, including these estimates is better than excluding sediment dynamics from the EFlows assessment entirely.

4.6.5 Field data collection

Project-directed EFlows assessments will almost always be based primarily on existing data and knowledge, as the project development timelines are too short to allow the collection of meaningful ecological datasets. Nonetheless, field visits are an essential component of any EFlows assessment. Beyond data collection, they provide an opportunity to engage with local communities, exchange knowledge about the ecosystem, build a shared understanding, and place the study area in its real-world context.

Field data collection typically focuses on

(i) topographical and hydraulic surveys to improve modeling efforts,
(ii) characterization of aquatic habitats,
(iii) understanding subsistence and other uses of the ecosystem,
(iv) developing an understanding of the overall ecological context of a proposed project, and
(v) collecting data to ground-truth remote images or historical data and information.

The level of detail is largely dependent on the number, quality, and subject matter of other studies in the area, and the detail at which an EFlows assessment is conducted.

4.6.6 Specialist studies and setup of the assessment framework

4.6.6.1 Literature review

Collecting empirical data on causal relationships within the typical time frames of project-related EFlows assessments is not feasible. Therefore, much of the necessary information for evaluating EFlows must be derived from scientific literature. This includes life-history data; connections between biota and habitats; and ecosystem responses to changes in water, sediment flows, and migration patterns. A thorough literature review is a fundamental component of any EFlows assessment.

4.6.6.2 Status and trends

4.6.6.2.1 Baseline condition

Most EFlows assessments are based on defining a reference condition, as changes in ecosystem condition are measured relative to it. In many cases, the baseline condition at the time of the study—describing the ecosystem condition as it is at that time—is used as the reference point. In other cases, change is measured against the estimated "natural" condition. In disturbed ecosystems, this requires reconstruction of a hypothetical natural condition to use as the reference condition (e.g., Du Preez and Rowntree 2006; Dube et al. 2015).

The description of the reference condition should consider hydrology, hydraulics, geomorphology, water quality, habitats, and associated biota.

4.6.6.2.2 Past condition

Past and ongoing impacts on a river provide valuable context for understanding the baseline condition, the historical pressures on the river ecosystem, and its responses to those pressures. A past-trends assessment is also beneficial for identifying opportunities to reduce these pressures and for calibrating the models used in the EFlows assessment.

4.6.7 Reporting

The EFlows assessment report should include:

(i) A well-organized and transparent evaluation of potential impacts on aquatic ecosystems.
(ii) A clear description of the methods applied.
(iii) A summary of the development or flow scenarios that were assessed.
(iv) The predicted effects on ecosystem health for each scenario.
(v) The expected impacts on social and community uses of the aquatic system.
(vi) The data and evidence supporting the assessment's conclusions, with references.
(vii) Specific, measurable targets to guide future monitoring efforts.

EFlows is a specialized field, and the EFlows assessment report must undergo peer review to ensure the methods used and the findings presented are technically and scientifically robust.

4.6.8 Decision on environmental flows and setting targets

Determining an EFlows regime is ultimately a societal decision, informed by technical data and ideally based on stakeholder-selected scenarios (section 4.6.2). As such, EFlows should be the result of thorough discussion, political negotiation, and social consensus achieved through stakeholder engagement (Vos 2020). Once a scenario is chosen, the specific hydrological, ecological, and social targets can then be established, grounded in the technical findings of the EFlows assessment.

4.6.9 Environmental flows management plan

The environmental flows management plan (EFMP) captures the results of the EFlows assessment, incorporates the tools and models developed during the process, and formalizes the agreements made regarding a project's EFlows commitments.

The EFMP should follow adaptive management principles and include, at a minimum:

(i) the agreed-upon EFlows;
(ii) EFlows targets;
(iii) a monitoring plan (section 4.6.10);
(iv) implementation roles and responsibilities;
(v) financing arrangements for EFMP execution; and
(vi) a schedule for review and adjustment, as needed.

Note: Finalizing the EFMP requires a decision on which scenario will be adopted as the EFlows regime.

4.6.10 Monitoring

An EFlows assessment is incomplete without post-implementation monitoring. Monitoring frameworks should be established to track river conditions over time, enabling adaptive management. This approach allows strategies to be adjusted in response to real-time data, enhancing ecosystem resilience and project performance. The components making up a monitoring program are project-, river-, and target-specific (section 4.6.8). Table 7 outlines some of the most common aspects and provides an idea of monitoring frequency.

Post-implementation monitoring is crucial. It helps ensure agreed EFlows are being met, checks if ecosystem targets are achieved, and addresses any initial issues. It also provides valuable data for future EFlows assessments.

For this to be effective, monitoring data should be collected regularly, quality-checked, analyzed, and clearly reported. Reports and data should be available for periodic audits and external review, supporting adaptive management and future EFlows assessments.

Table 7: Outline of an Environmental Flows Monitoring Program

Discipline	Data	Recommended Frequency of Data Collection
Hydrology	River hydrology at key points upstream and downstream of project(s)	Daily or sub-daily as appropriate
	Inflows to project(s)	
	Releases from project(s)	
	Diversions from project(s)	
Hydraulics	Channel dimensions at gauging and EFlows monitoring sites	6-monthly
Sediments	Suspended sediment concentrations and grain size	Daily or sub-daily as appropriate
	Bed sediment composition at gauging stations and EFlows monitoring sites	Every 6 months, before and after the wet season
Geomorphology	Aquatic habitat mappinga	6-monthly
	Fixed point photography at gauging stations and EFlows monitoring sites	
Water quality	Electrical conductivity, temperature, and dissolved oxygen at gauging stations and EFlows monitoring sites	Daily or sub-daily, as appropriate
	Monitoring of other water quality parameters, as appropriate for the project under consideration, e.g., biological oxygen demand should be measured downstream of sewage outfalls	Weekly or monthly, as appropriate
Algae and diatoms	Species present	6-monthly
	Abundance	
Instream and riparian vegetation	Species present	
	Abundance	
	Recruitment	
Macroinvertebrates	Families present	
	Abundance	

continued on next page

Table 7 *continued*

Discipline	Data	Recommended Frequency of Data Collection
Fish	Species present	
	Tail length	
	Health	
	Gravid females	
Other animals as appropriate	Abundance and community composition	
Affected people	Damage to infrastructure or fields	
	Fish catch data	
	Lived experience	

Eflows = Environmental Flows.

[a] Aquatic habitat mapping is the process of identifying and recording different types of habitats found in river ecosystems, e.g., riffles, pools, runs.

Source: Authors.

4.6.10.1 Establishing a baseline dataset

A reliable baseline dataset is essential for protecting developers from unfounded claims and serving as a reference for detecting any changes caused by the project.

The EFlows monitoring program should begin at least 2 years before project construction starts, allowing time to establish a baseline dataset that reflects the natural variability of the river system before any project-related impacts occur. While data from assessments such as an ESIA and EFlows can contribute to this baseline, they are typically insufficient on their own to provide a comprehensive and defensible dataset.

4.6.10.2 Reporting

Annual EFlows monitoring reports should include (UNEP 2020):

(i) implementation of EFlows procedures analysis and compliance, including:

(ii) documentation of issues or problems related to implementation, if any, and suggested solutions;

(iii) hydrological analysis and compliance, including (at the appropriate time step, but no greater than daily):

   (a) statistical summaries of the releases from impoundments, including percent compliance with the EFlows, annual and seasonal flow duration curves, and duration curves of rates of water flow change, and a breakdown of the calculated flows;

(i) measured river condition targets analysis and compliance, including

   (a) comparative analysis of baseline and monitoring data, and

   (b) trend analysis of monitoring data.

4.6.11 Adaptive Management

Adaptive management is vital as it allows for the adjustment of EFlows based on ongoing monitoring and evaluation and learning by doing (Williams 2011). This is particularly true given the typical dearth of reliable and long-term information and data for the ecosystems affected by ADB-supported projects.

4.7 Construction and commissioning impacts

During the construction phase of projects that impact rivers, the effects on the broader river ecosystem can be significant. These impacts may be short-term or persist throughout the operational life of the dam, including:

(i) Redirection of river flow to facilitate construction activities.
(ii) Increased sedimentation caused by disturbances to the riverbed and banks, which can affect water quality, harm aquatic life, and limit light penetration, hindering plant growth.
(iii) Extraction of construction materials from the riverbed outside the proposed inundation area and from tributaries, which destroys habitats.
(iv) Disposal of muck into or alongside the river, tributaries, and drainage lines.
(v) Pollution from construction materials, chemicals, and waste such as oils, lubricants, cement, and other hazardous substances.
(vi) Temporary or permanent disruption of migration patterns for riverine species.
(vii) Noise and vibration pollution from heavy machinery, blasting, and other activities, potentially impacting riverine and terrestrial species.
(viii) In tropical regions, filling a reservoir can release methane, a potent greenhouse gas.

Similarly, during the testing and commissioning of projects such as dams or hydropower plants, test releases should be carefully evaluated for their downstream impact, ensuring that agreed-upon EFlows allocations are consistently maintained. Interrupting river flows can cause irreversible damage to the river ecosystem once a project has been fully commissioned.

To avoid or mitigate these impacts, careful planning, strict adherence to EFlows provisions, robust environmental oversight, and monitoring are essential, along with the use of best practices. Destruction of in-channel habitats outside the immediate project area, including tributaries and habitats linked to drainage lines, should be strongly discouraged, as these areas serve as refuges for riverine and other wildlife.

APPENDIX 1
Case Studies and Best Practices

A1.1 Environmental Flows assessments on ADB projects

A1.1.1 Brenwe Hydroelectric Power Project, Brenwe River, Vanuatu

The Brenwe Hydroelectric Power Project (HPP) is a 400-kilowatt (kW) project proposed for the Brenwe River, Malekula, Vanuatu. The design and planned operation fall within the definition of a "true run-of-river" hydropower project (World Bank Group 2018): *"Hydropower projects that release downstream into the same river, with a short or no diversion, have 48 hours or less dry season storage and do not make peaking-power releases."*

There is a 1-kilometer (km) diversion between the weir and tailrace, which includes "a 30-m [meter] high waterfall and two other cascades >3 m high. A weir from a previous power scheme is also present" (Wildlands 2021).

The average annual flow (AAF) for the Brenwe River is 0.78 cubic meters per second (m^3/s).[1] The flow is stable for much of the year, although there are some higher flows in the wet season. *"Flood peaks are sharp and storm runoff declines rapidly as surface runoff appears to infiltrate into subterranean storage for slow release during dry periods and throughout the dry season" (Wildlands 2021).*

The study team used the Low Resolution EFlows Method, the Tennant Method, combined with sediment and connectivity assessments. Importantly, the EFlows study was a repeat of an earlier "EFlows assessment," which used the 10% rule or similar, and suggested that 0.8 m^3/s would protect the river ecosystem. Reviewers rejected this, and the EFlows assessment had to be redone.

Tennant is quick and easy to apply and provides an easily understood single number or monthly or seasonal values. It is based on relationships derived from rivers in Montana, United States (US), which differ from those in the study area, and it does not consider the baseline status of the river ecosystem, but it can be conservative if applied correctly, which was the case here. The percentages of AFF recommended by Tennant to achieve different objectives are given in Table AA. 1.

The EFlows study resulted in a recommendation for a release from Brenwe HPP of 0.31 m^3/s into the dewatered reach (Anon 2021). This equates to <99th percentile (Q^{99}) on the flow duration curve provided. River flows are constant throughout the year, so the <Q^{99} is nowhere near as extreme as it would be in a flashier system.

Based on the 0.31 m^3/s and the AAF provided (0.78 m^3/s), the recommended EFlows for the dewatered reach are about 40% of the AFF. Thus, according to Tennant (1976), this should maintain the dewatered reach in somewhere between a good and excellent condition, provided the river also received some flushing flows (Table AA.1) based on the inherent (and untested) assumption that the Brenwe River responds similarly to flow manipulations as rivers in Montana, US.

[1] AAF used to be in keeping with Tennant Method.

Table A1: Tennant Method: Percentage of Average Annual Flow Required to Achieve Different Objectives

Objective	Recommended Percentage of Average Annual Flow[a] October–March (%)	April–September (%)
Flushing or maximum flows	200	200
Optimum range of AAF	60–100	60–100
Percentage AAF Required to Maintain a Required River Condition		
Outstanding	40	60
Excellent	30	50
Good	20	40
Fair or degrading	10	30
Poor or minimum	10	10
Severe degradation	10–zero flow	10–zero flow

AAF = average annual flow.

[a] AAF expressed as instantaneous flow; US seasonal-divisions used.

Source: D. L. Tennant. 1976. Instream flow regimens for fish, wildlife, recreation and related environmental resources.

A1.1.2 Gulpur Hydro Power Project, Poonch River, Pakistan

The Poonch River flows for about 85 km before entering the Mangla reservoir. This entire stretch lies within the Poonch River Mahaseer National Park, an area recognized for its scenic landscapes and high levels of fish endemism, including the endangered Mahaseer (*Tor putitora*). Limited funding for park management, along with sediment extraction, harmful fishing practices, nutrient enrichment from effluent discharges, and removal of riparian vegetation, places significant pressure on the river ecosystem.

The 100-megawatt (MW) Gulpur Hydropower Project (GHPP) was developed in the park by Mira Power Ltd. from the Republic of Korea. The initial design of the HPP included a 35 m weir, a 3.1 km headrace tunnel connecting the intake to the powerhouse, and a tailrace that would discharge water back into the river about 6 km downstream of the weir. The powerhouse would comprise three Francis 33.33-MW turbines with a minimum operational discharge of 33.0 m^3/s. The design "EFlows" were planned as a minimum release of 4.0 m^3/s compared with the baseline minimum 5-day dry-season discharge of 20.4 m^3/s. The weir would not materially alter the wet-season flows, but would affect the dry-season onset, duration, and discharge magnitude between the weir and the tailrace under base-power operation, and much of the remaining river under peaking-power operation.

The environmental and social impact assessment (ESIA) initially completed for the GHPP was rejected because the Poonch River is both a national park and a critical habitat, and a high-resolution EFlows assessment was recommended.

The DRIFT EFlows assessment method was used to evaluate >20 scenarios comprising different permutations of minimum releases from 4.0–16.0 m3/s.; three future levels of management aimed at reducing the non-flow related pressures on the system; peaking versus baseflow operation; options for reducing the distance of the de-watered section of river between the weir and tailrace; and options for turbine selection. All the scenarios considered the effects of trapping bedload and suspended sediments in the Gulpur reservoir, as well as the barrier effect of the weir on fish movement between downstream overwintering areas and upstream breeding areas.

For each scenario, the outcome was expressed as an overall ecosystem condition in different river reaches using an integrity range from A to F and as semi-quantitative changes for 16 indicators of ecosystem condition, including fish. The implication for power generation was also provided for each scenario (using a Scenario Generation Model; main text, section 4.6.3).

The EFlows assessment showed that even without the GHPP, the river ecosystem and biodiversity would continue to decline in the absence of focused management interventions, and that with the GHPP, there would be a net positive effect on overall ecosystem condition upstream, provided high-level conservation protection (funded by hydropower generation) was also implemented. It also showed that increasing the minimum releases from 4.0 m^3/s to 8.0 m^3/s would not significantly improve the outcome for the river section between the weir and the tailrace, and that downstream of the tailrace, peaking power operations would significantly adversely affect both overall condition and biodiversity.

The full range of scenarios was presented to the stakeholders, comprising local communities, government officials, the developer, Pakistan Power Authority, and representatives from the lending organizations, including the Asian Development Bank and the International Finance Corporation (IFC).

The results of the EFlows Assessment underpinned the following decision:

(i) forgo peaking power generation;

(ii) relocate the GHPP weir closer to the power house to, inter alia, reduce the dewatered section from about 6 km to about 1 km;

(iii) release a minimum discharge of 4.0 m^3/s for the (shortened) section of river between the weir and tailrace;

(iv) select different turbines that would allow greater operating flexibility under low-flow conditions;

(v) implement a management and finance structure for high levels of protection in the Poonch River National Park, as this offered better overall biodiversity protection than increasing the EFlows release above 4.0 m^3/s.

Post-project monitoring of the river, the operation of GHPP, and the implementation of the management plan have demonstrated that these provisions have been largely successful (HBP 2025).

A1.2 Key lessons from EFlows implementation

There are a substantial number of examples of successful EFlows implementation (e.g., WWF 2017, Table A2). The key lessons from these include:

(i) General Principles

- (a) Healthy rivers are essential for delivering long-term ecosystem services and sustainability.
- (b) Broad stakeholder concern—including from governments, nongovernment organizations, and the public—can drive the adoption of EFlows.
- (c) EFlows enhance river resilience to future pressures.
- (d) Clear, well-defined goals are critical to successful EFlows programs.

(ii) Institutional Factors
   (a) Strong political and institutional support is key to success.
   (b) Collaboration across all levels of government, civil society, and stakeholders is essential.
   (c) Adequate resources, capacity, and trust among stakeholders and regulators are necessary for implementation.

(iii) EFlows Assessment
   (a) Challenges in assessment and implementation can be addressed with the right approach.
   (b) Holistic, ecosystem-based, and high-resolution assessment methods are best practice.
   (c) Local knowledge, uncertainties, and knowledge gaps should be integrated, especially during implementation.
   (d) Transparency in tools and methods builds trust.
   (e) Defining EFlows in specific, measurable terms (e.g., flow magnitude, timing) improves clarity and implementation.
   (f) Scientific justification and trade-off analyses are crucial for stakeholder buy-in.
   (g) Project designs should account for environmental, social, and economic factors.
   (h) Communications should be science-based but tailored for various audiences, including non-technical stakeholders.

(iv) Monitoring and Adaptive Management
   (a) Monitoring and adaptive management are essential for evaluating outcomes and adjusting strategies.
   (b) Sustainable funding is necessary for implementation and monitoring efforts.
   (c) Effective monitoring depends on reliable infrastructure and timely data management and sharing.

Table A2: Examples of Where Environmental Flows Are Being Implemented

Continent	Case Study	Detailed Information Available From:
Europe	River Kennet (England)	WWF (2017)
	River Pang (England)	Acreman (2000, 2001)
	Redgrave and Lopham Fen (England)	Fojt (1994)
Asia	Lake Chilika (India)	Hirji and Davis (2009)
	Ganga and Ramganga rivers (India)	WWF (2017)
	Yangtze River (PRC)	WWF (2017)
	Yellow River (PRC)	Zhang et al. (2016)
	Poonch River (Pakistan)	Brown et al. (2017)
Oceania	Murray-Darling Basin (Australia)	WWF (2017)
Africa	Mara River (Kenya, Tanzania)	WWF and Lake Victoria Basin Commission (2010)
	Kilombero and Rufiji rivers (Tanzania)	CDM Smith (2016)
	Highlands Water Project (Lesotho)	Hirji and Davis (2009)
	Crocodile River, Kruger National Park	WWF (2017)
	Kafue River (Zambia)	Kalumba and Nyirenda (2017)
	Phongolo River (South Africa)	Dube *et al.* (2015)
	Senegal River (Mali, Mauritania, Senegal, Guinea)	Hirji and Davis (2009)

continued on next page

Table A2 *continued*

Continent	Case Study	Detailed Information Available From:
South America	Rio São Francisco (Brazil)	Brambilla et al. (2017)
	Paraná River (Brazil)	Souza et al. (2008), Agostinho et al. (2008)
North America	Colorado River (US, Mexico)	CWCB (2012)
	Deschutes River (US)	Golden and Aylward (2006)
	Columbia River (US, Canada)	Dyson et al. (2008), BC Hydro (2017)
	San Pedro Mezquital River (Mexico)	WWF (2017)
	Athabasca River (Canada)	WWF (2011)
	Sustainable Rivers Program (US)	WWF (2017)
	Peace River (US)	Locke et al. (2008)

CWCB = Colorado Water Conservation Board, PRC = People's Republic of China, US = United States, WWF = World Wide Fund for Nature.

Sources: WWF. 2017. Listen to the river: Lessons from a global review of Environmental Flows success stories; see Reference section in the main text for publication details.

Figure A1: Location of Examples of Where EFlows Are Being Implemented

Source: WWF for Nature. 2017. Listen to the river: Lessons from a global review of Environmental Flows success stories.

APPENDIX 2
Generic Templates for Terms of Reference

Appendix B provides generic templates for the terms of reference (TORs) corresponding to each of the resolution levels described in the main document. Guidance on the appropriate environmental flows (EFlows) assessment level for a project is provided in the main text, section 4.3.

These templates serve as a starting point for developing project-specific TORs, but should be adapted to reflect the characteristics of the project. In particular:

(i) The downstream extent of project impacts will determine the number of EFlows assessment sites or zones required. This depends on the project's location and design, the nature of the river and its network, and the presence of other developments in the basin.

(ii) The estimated project duration is highly dependent on the project start date, as field data collection in rivers is strongly influenced by seasonal conditions. Ideally, most of the fieldwork should be conducted during the dry season, and in regions with significant snowfall, during the late dry season. Conducting initial fieldwork during the wet season is less desirable due to access difficulties, reduced visibility, increased safety risks, and challenges in site selection.

(iii) The scope and duration of hydrological data preparation are highly dependent on the availability of long-term daily hydrological data for the river system.

(iv) Hydrodynamic modeling is necessary only if the project is expected to cause rapid, large-scale changes in the downstream river, such as those resulting from hydropeaking or sediment flushing.

(v) The scope and duration of biological sampling depend on the availability of existing data for the river system.

(vi) All three templates focus on river ecosystems; projects that may affect other aquatic systems, such as lakes or estuaries, will require TORs expanded to address those environments.

A2.1 Low-resolution Environmental Flows assessment

Low-resolution EFlows assessments are intended for use in low-risk projects that

(i) involve abstractions ≤25% of the mean volume of the three lowest months;

(ii) have negligible impacts on water quality, sediment transport, or migration patterns;

(iii) are not in a protected area; and

(iv) do not affect natural or critical habitat.

A2.1.1 Background

The [Project Name] is expected to cause minimal alteration of river flows, with no critical/natural habitat identified and limited upstream or downstream socioeconomic reliance on flows. A low-resolution environmental flows (EFlows) study is required to ensure compliance with ADB's Environmental and Social Framework (ESF) and good international practice.

Refer to ADB's *Guidance Note on Environmental Flows Assessment and Management for ADB-Financed Projects (2024)* for the definition of EFlows and guidance on conducting a low-resolution EFlows assessment.

A2.1.2 Objectives

To define a hydrological EFlows regime that will mitigate project impacts on key ecological functions and ecosystem services in the downstream river.

A2.1.3 Approach

Primarily desktop-based analysis supplemented by targeted field verification. Stakeholder engagement is limited to key agencies and major water users.

A2.1.4 Scope of Work

The consultant will:

1. Review available topographical, hydrological, ecological, and socioeconomic data, and remote imagery.
2. Delineate the downstream river, and select appropriate EFlows assessment sites to represent, at a minimum:
    a. any river reach that is expected to be dewatered; and
    b. downstream of the project, to the extent that the impacts on the hydrology and sediment regime and migratory paths reach.
3. Identify and motivate an appropriate rapid EFlows assessment method for application based on the outcomes of 1 and 2 above, the approach outlined in section A2.1.3.
4. Undertake a basic EFlows analysis to estimate dry-season low flows and seasonal variation needed to maintain the downstream river, and identify any other likely flow-related impacts, such as those to the sediment regime or migration patterns.
5. Recommend a hydrological EFlows regime and operational rules that maintain seasonal patterns
6. Define basic monitoring indicators and outline a monitoring program.

A2.1.5 Deliverables

(i) Inception report.
(ii) Technical memorandum with EFlows recommendations, operational rules, and monitoring indicators.
(iii) Final report (month 3).
(iv) Presentation to client and other stakeholders (month 3).

A2.1.6 Estimated duration

3 months.

Personnel requirements and person-months

Position	Person-Months	Key Tasks
EFlows practitioner	1.5–3	Select method, compile required data, undertake assessment, oversee deliverables
Hydrologist	0.5–1.0	Generate hydrological time series data for the assessment, and indicate how the project will affect seasonal volumes and patterns
Total person-months = 2–4		

A2.2 Medium-Resolution EFlows Assessment

Medium-resolution EFlows assessments are intended for use in *moderate-risk* projects that:

(i) are situated on rivers with low social dependency;

(ii) have a reservoir storage volume ≤100% (natural) mean annual runoff (MAR) of the host river;

(iii) are not part of a cascade of developments; and

(iv) will not result in seasonal, rapid changes in discharge in the downstream river (e.g., hydropeaking).

A2.2.1 Background

The [Project Name] is expected to moderately alter seasonal hydrological patterns, sediment transport, and/or aquatic connectivity. A medium-resolution environmental flows (EFlows) study is required to ensure compliance with ADB's Environmental and Social Framework (ESF) and good international practice.

Refer to ADB's *Guidance Note on Environmental Flows Assessment and Management for ADB-Financed Projects* for the definition of EFlows and guidance on conducting a medium-resolution EFlows assessment.

A2.2.2 Objectives

To generate EFlows information and data that support the selection of an EFlows regime and associated operating rules that balance project operations with ecological integrity, sediment transport, migration pathways, and community livelihoods.

A2.2.3 Scope of Work

The consultant will:

1. Review available hydrological, ecological, and socioeconomic data.
2. Liaise with the client to obtain an understanding of the intended design and operation of the proposed project.
3. Identify sensitive aquatic habitats and key species and estimate the potential downstream extent of impacts.
4. Identify and motivate an appropriate medium-resolution EFlows assessment method for application.
5. Select 2–3 EFlows assessment sites or zones. These should comprise at least one site/zone upstream of the project, and 1–2 sites/zones downstream of the project to the extent of the project's influence on the flow of water, sediments, and migratory species.

6. Conduct at least one multidisciplinary field survey (hydrology, hydraulics, sediment, ecology, water quality, socioeconomic) to gather data on habitats and species to inform inputs to the EFlows assessments, and to gain an understanding of subsistence and other uses of the ecosystem.
7. Compile daily hydrological time series of about 20 years to represent the baseline and, to the extent possible, the natural hydrology of the study river at each of the EFlows sites/zones.
8. Model or estimate a time series for the same period for suspended sediment.
9. Select a suite of appropriate habitat, biotic, and social indicators.
10. Undertake a literature review to establish, to the extent possible:
    a. geomorphological processes supporting riverine habitats;
    b. the life history requirements of species found in the river; and
    c. the impacts of social use on the ecosystem, and potential mitigation thereof.
11. Evaluate the likely impact on migration of any barriers, with and without mitigation.
12. Liaise with the client to develop a set of operational scenarios based on the proposed design and operation of the project for evaluation.
13. Model the design and operation of the project to determine downstream impacts on the hydrological and sediment regimes, and on longitudinal and lateral connectivity.
14. Undertake a basic EFlows analysis of the scenarios developed and describe the expected impact on the indicators selected in #9.
15. Present the scenario outcomes to the client for evaluation.
16. Consult with the client and other stakeholders to facilitate a decision on an EFlows regime and associated operating rules.
17. Compile an EFlows management plan (EFMP) that follows adaptive management principles and includes:
    a. the agreed-upon EFlows;
    b. additional agreed mitigatory actions;
    c. EFlows targets;
    d. a basic monitoring plan;
    e. implementation roles and responsibilities;
    f. financing arrangements for EFMP execution; and
    g. a schedule for review and adjustment, as needed.

A2.2.4 Methodology

The consultant must identify, motivate for, and describe, as appropriate:

(i) models and modeling used to:
  (a) develop natural and baseline hydrological time series,
  (b) provide ecohydraulic data at EFlows sites,
  (c) model project operations to generate scenarios for evaluation; and

(ii) an EFlows assessment method that can be implemented at a medium resolution to provide the level of integration and detail required to meet the project objectives.

A2.2.5 Deliverables

(i) Inception Report
(ii) Hydrology Report
(iii) Ecohydraulics Report
(iv) Supporting Specialists Report: Ecology
(v) Supporting Specialists Report: Social
(vi) EFlows Assessment Report
(vii) Decision on EFlows Memorandum
(viii) Draft Environmental Flow Management Plan.

A2.2.6 Estimated duration

6–12 months.

A2.2.7 Personnel requirements and person-months

These estimates are based on approximately 2–3 EFlows sites: one upstream and 1–2 downstream of the project.

Position	Person-months	Key Tasks
EFlows practitioner	2–3	Select method, compile required data, undertake assessment, oversee deliverables, estimate time series of suspended sediments for natural, baseline, and operational scenarios, guide client in understanding scenario outputs, and develop an EFMP
Hydrologist	1–2	Generate hydrological time series data for the assessment, and indicate how the project will affect seasonal volumes and patterns
Fish passage specialist	1	Evaluate implications for fish passage of project design, including potential fish passage systems
Scenario modeler	0.5–1	Model the design and operation of the project to determine downstream impacts on the hydrological regimes
Water quality specialist	0.5–1	Water quality assessment, status and trends analysis, flows dependency analysis, and evaluation of potential management impacts
Geomorphologist	1–1.5	Field data collection, literature review, indicator selection, status and trends analysis, flows dependency analysis, and evaluation of potential management impacts
Botanist	1–1.5	
Macroinvertebrate ecologist	1–1.5	
Fish ecologist	1–1.5	
Social specialist	1–1.5	
GIS technician	0.5–1	Maps and spatial analyses
Total person-months = 9–15.5		

EFMP = environmental flows management plan, GIS = geographic information system.

A2.3 High-Resolution EFlows Study

High-resolution EFlows assessments are intended for use in potentially high-risk projects that fulfil one or more of the following criteria. They:

(i) are situated on rivers with high social dependency;
(ii) have a reservoir storage volume >100% of the natural MAR of the host river;
(iii) are part of a cascade of developments;
(iv) are in a protected area, natural, or critical habitat; and/or
(v) may result in seasonal, rapid changes in discharge in the downstream river, e.g., hydropeaking.

A2.3.1 Background

The [*Project Name*] is in a sensitive basin with critical and/or natural habitats, threatened species, and communities heavily dependent on riverine resources. It is expected to alter seasonal hydrological patterns, sediment transport, and/or aquatic connectivity. A high-resolution environmental flows (EFlows) study is required to ensure compliance with ADB's Environmental and Social Framework (ESF) and international good practice.

Refer to ADB's *Guidance Note on Environmental Flows Assessment and Management for ADB-Financed Projects* for the definition of EFlows and guidance on conducting a high-resolution EFlows assessment.

A2.3.2 Objectives

To generate EFlows information and data that support the selection of a holistic EFlows regime and associated operating rules that balance, as far as possible, project operations with ecological integrity, sediment transport, migration pathways, and community livelihoods.

A2.3.3 Scope of Work

The consultant will:

1. Review available hydrological, ecological, and socioeconomic data.
2. Liaise with the client to obtain an understanding of the intended design and operation of the proposed project.
3. Identify sensitive aquatic habitats and key species and estimate the potential downstream extent of impacts.
4. Identify and motivate an appropriate high-resolution EFlows assessment method for application.
5. Select 5–6 EFlows assessment sites or zones. These should comprise at least one site/zone upstream of the project, and 4–5 sites/zones downstream of the project to the extent of the project's influence on the flow of water, sediments, and migratory species.
6. Conduct at least two seasonal multidisciplinary field surveys (hydrology, hydraulics, sediment, ecology, water quality, socioeconomic) to gather data on habitats and species to inform inputs to the EFlows assessments, to gain an understanding of subsistence and other uses of the ecosystem and to evaluate the potential for reducing the impact of social use on the system through management and other initiatives.
7. Compile daily hydrological time series of about 30 years to represent the baseline and, to the extent possible, the natural hydrology of the study river at each of the EFlows sites/zones.

8. Model or estimate a time series for the same period for suspended sediment.
9. Select a suite of appropriate habitat, biotic, and social indicators.
10. Undertake a literature review to establish, to the extent possible:
    a. geomorphological processes supporting the riverine habitats;
    b. the life history requirements of species found in the river; and
    c. the impacts of social use on the ecosystem, and potential mitigation thereof.
11. Evaluate the likely impact on migration of any barriers, with and without mitigation.
12. Liaise with the client to develop a set of operational scenarios based on the proposed design and operation of the project for evaluation, which include variations in:
    a. hydrology;
    b. sediment delivery;
    c. migration passages, e.g., fish passages; and
    d. levels of management of social use.
13. Model the design and operation of the project to determine downstream impacts on the hydrological and sediment regimes, and on longitudinal and lateral connectivity.
14. Undertake a basic EFlows analysis of the scenarios developed and describe the expected impact on the indicators selected in #9.
15. Present the scenario outcomes to the client for evaluation.
16. Consult with the client and other stakeholders to
    a. facilitate a decision on an EFlows regime, and associated operating rules; and
    b. develop adaptive management and offset strategies.
17. Compile an EFlows management plan (EFMP) that follows adaptive management principles and includes:
    a. the agreed-upon EFlows;
    b. additional agreed mitigatory actions;
    c. EFlows targets;
    d. a monitoring plan;
    e. implementation roles and responsibilities;
    f. financing arrangements for EFMP execution; and
    g. a schedule for review and adjustment, as needed.
17. Facilitate extensive stakeholder consultations, including transboundary dialogue, if required.

A2.3.4 Methodology

The consultant must identify, motivate for, and describe, as appropriate:

(i) models and modeling used to:
    (a) develop natural and baseline hydrological time series,
    (b) provide ecohydraulic data at EFlows sites,
    (c) route releases downstream,
    (d) model project operations to generate scenarios for evaluation; and
(ii) an EFlows assessment method that can be implemented at a high resolution to provide the level of integration and detail required to meet the project objectives.

A2.3.5 Deliverables

(i) Inception Report
(ii) Hydrology Report
(iii) Ecohydraulics and Hydrodynamic Modeling Report
(iv) Supporting Specialists Report: Ecology and Social
(v) EFlows Assessment Report
(vi) Decision on EFlows Memorandum
(vii) Draft Environmental Flow Management Plan.

A2.3.6 Estimated duration

12–16 months.

A2.3.7 Personnel requirements and person-months

These estimates are based on approximately 5–6 EFlows sites: one upstream and 4–5 downstream of the project.

Position	Person-Months	Key Tasks
EFlows Practitioner	3–4	Select method, compile required data, undertake assessment, oversee deliverables, guide client in understanding scenario outputs, and develop an EFMP
Hydrologist	1–2	Generate hydrological time series data for the assessment, and indicate how the project will affect seasonal volumes and patterns
Hydraulician	2–4	Model site and reach hydraulics/hydrodynamics needed to translate discharge data (m^3/s) into more ecologically meaningful parameters, such as depth, velocity, shear stress, wetted area
Sediment specialist	1–2	Generate a time series of suspended sediments for natural, baseline, and operational scenarios
Fish passage specialist	1–1.5	Evaluate implications for fish passage of project design, including potential fish passage systems
Scenario modeler	0.5–1	Model the design and operation of the project to determine downstream impacts on the hydrological regimes
Water quality specialist	1–1.5	Water quality assessment, status and trends analysis, flows dependency analysis, and evaluation of potential management impacts
Geomorphologist	1.5–2	Field data collection, literature review, indicator selection, status and trends analysis, flows dependency analysis, and evaluation of potential management impacts
Botanist	1.5–2	
Macroinvertebrate ecologist	1.5–2	
Fish ecologist	1.5–2	
Social specialist	1.5–2	
GIS technician	0.5–1	Maps and spatial analyses
Total person-months = 17.5–27		

EFMP = environmental flows management plan, GIS = geographic information system, m^3/s = cubic meters per second.

References

M. Acreman. (ed). 2001. Guidelines for the Sustainable Management of Groundwater-fed Catchments. Groundwater and River Resources Programme on a European Scale (GRAPES), European Commission. ENV4-CT95-0186. Centre for Ecology and Hydrology.

M. Acreman. 2001. Towards the sustainable management of groundwater-fed catchments in Europe. In Regional Management of Water Resources. Proceedings of an International Symposium (Symposium S2) Held During the Sixth Scientific Assembly of the International Association of Hydrological Sciences (IAHS) at Maastricht, The Netherlands, from 18 to 27 July 2001. 268. IAHS.

A. A. Agostinho et al. 2008. Application of the ecohydrological concept for sustainable development of tropical floodplains: the case of the upper Paraná River Basin. *Ecohydrology and Hydrobiology.* 8. pp. 205–223.

Anon. 2021. VPMU plan to demonstrate compliance with ADB SPS on habitat mitigation measures for the Brenwe River.

Asian Development Bank (ADB). 2024. Environmental and Social Framework (ESF).

V. Barbarossa et al. 2020. Impacts of current and future large dams on the geographic range connectivity of freshwater fish worldwide. *Environmental Sciences.* 117 (7). pp. 3648–3655.

J. Baron et al. 2002. Meeting ecological and societal needs for freshwater. *Ecological applications.* 12 (5). pp. 1247–1260.

M. Brambilla, A. S. Fontes, and Y. Medeiros. 2017. Cost-benefit analysis of reservoir operation scenarios considering environmental flows for the lower stretch of the São Francisco River (Brazil). *Scientific/Technical Article. RBRH 22.*

C. Brown et al. 2017. Achieving an environmentally sustainable outcome for the Gulpur hydropower project in the Poonch River Mahaseer National Park, Pakistan. *Sustainable Water Resources Management.* 5. pp. 611–628.

H. Bukhari et al. 2025. Exploring expert-derived driver-response relationships used in EFlows assessments in southern Africa. Water SA. 51.

CDM Smith Engineers. 2016. Environmental Flows in the Rufiji River Basin assessed from the perspective of planned development in the Kilombera and Lower Rufiji sub-basins. Report to the United States Agency for International Development.

Colorado Water Conservation Board (CWCB). 2012. Colorado River Water Availability Study. Phase 1 Report.

L. Du Preez and K. M. Rowntree. 2006. Assessment of the geomorphological reference condition: An application for resource directed measures and the river health programme. *WRC Report.* 1306 (1) 06.

T. Dube et al. 2015. The case for Environmental Flows determination for the Phongolo River, South Africa. *African Journal of Aquatic Sciences.* 40(3). pp. 269–276.

M. Dyson, G. Bergkamp, and J. Scanlon, J. (eds.) 2008. *The essentials of environmental flows, 2nd Edition.* Reprint, International Union for the Conservation of Nature (IUCN).

EDF and GMR. 2023. Upper Karnali Hydropower Project. Rapid Cumulative Impact Assessment Report.

European Water Framework Directive. 2000. DIRECTIVE 2000/60/EC OF THE EUROPEAN PARLIAMENT AND OF THE COUNCIL of 23 October 2000 establishing a framework for Community action in the field of water policy. Official Journal of the European Communities L 327/1.

J. Fojt. 1994. Dehydration and the threat to East Anglian fens, England. *Biological Conservation.* 69 (2): pp. 163–175.

J. A. Fowler et al. 2021. Disaggregated monthly hydrological models can outperform daily models in providing daily flow statistics and extrapolate well to a drying climate. *Journal of Hydrology.* 598. ISSN 0022–1694.

D. Golden and B. Aylward. 2006. Instream Flow in the Deschutes Basin: Monitoring, Status and Restoration Needs.

Government of British Columbia, BC Hydro. 2017. *Columbia River Water Use Planning*.

Hagler Bailly Pakistan. 2023. Environmental and Social Baseline Data Collection, EFlows Assessment, Rapid Cumulative Impact Assessment for Upper Karnali Hydropower Project. *Unpublished.* EDF.

Hagler Bailly Pakistan. 2025. Monitoring and Evaluation of the Biodiversity Action Plan for Gulpur Hydropower Project for Poonch River Mahseer National Park. Annual Monitoring Report for the reporting Year 2024. Report to Mira Power Limited. Report No. D5ME1GME.

R. Hirji and R. Davis. 2009. Environmental Flows in Water Resources, Policies, Plans and Projects. *Case Studies. Environment Department. World Bank.*

R. J. Hobbs and J. A. Harris. 2001. Restoration Ecology: Repairing the Earth's Ecosystems in the New Millennium. *Restoration Ecology. 9 (2). pp. 239-246.*

International Finance Corporation (IFC). 2013. Good Practice Handbook on Cumulative Impact Assessment and Management: Guidance for the Private Sector in Emerging Markets.

IFC. 2020. Cumulative Impact Assessment and Management: Hydropower Development in the Trishuli River Basin, Nepal. IFC.

K. Jorde. 1999. The Simulation Model CASIMIR as a Tool for Determining Ecologically Justified Minimum Flow Regulations. Presented at the conference *Problemkreis Pflichtwasserabgabe* held in Graz (June 21–23, 1999), published in proceedings by Euronatur.

M. Kalumba and E. Nyirenda. 2017. River flow availability for Environmental Flows allocation downstream of hydropower facilities in the Kafue Basin of Zambia. *Physics and Chemistry of the Earth.* 102. pp. 21–30.

J. M. King and C.A. Brown. 2018a. Environmental Flows, minimum flows and the mystery of ten percent. In: P. Gough and J. Royte. (eds). Sea to Source. Protection and restoration of fish migration in rivers worldwide. pp. 107-111. World Fish Migration Foundation.

J. M. King and C.A. Brown. 2018b. Environmental Flow Assessments Are Not Realizing Their Potential as an Aid to Basin Planning. *Frontiers of Environmental Science.*

A. U. Kumar and K. V. Jayakumar. 2020. Modelling of Environmental Flows requirements using hydraulic and habitation models. *Ecological Indicators.* 121.

A. Locke et al. 2008. *Integrated Approaches to Riverine Resource Management: Case Studies, Science, Law, People, and Policy.* Instream Flow Council.

S. Marsili-Libelli, E. Giusti, and A. Nocita. 2013. A new instream flow assessment method based on fuzzy habitat suitability and large scale river modelling. *Modelling and Software.* 41. pp. 27–38. .

Mekong River Commission. 2017. The Council Study: Study on the sustainable management and development of the Mekong River, including impacts of mainstream hydropower projects. BioRA Final Technical Report Series. Volume 4: Assessment of Planned Development Scenarios. Final Report.

C. F. Souza et al. 2008. *Ecohydrology towards the sustainable development: An approach based on South American case studies. Ecohydrology and Hydrobiology. 8. pp. 225-235.*

E. Stein et al. 2014. Hydromodification assessment and management in California. Technical Report 667. Southern California Coastal Water Research Project.

D. L. Tennant. 1976. Instream flow regimens for fish, wildlife, recreation and related environmental resources. *Fisheries.* 1 (4). pp. 6–10.

R. Tharme. 2003. A Global perspective on Environmental Flow Assessment: Emerging trends in the development and application of environmental flow methodologies for river. *River Research and Applications.* 19. pp. 397–441.

D. Tickner et al. *2020.* Bending the Curve of Global Freshwater Biodiversity Loss: An Emergency Recovery Plan. *BioScience.* 70 (4). pp. 330–342.

United Nations Environment Programme (UNEP). *2018.* WIOSAP Project Summary: Implementation of the Strategic Action Programme for the protection of the Western Indian Ocean from land-based sources and activities (WIO-SAP). UNEP.

UNEP-Nairobi Convention/Western Indian Ocean Marine Science Association. 2020. Guidelines for the Assessment of Environmental Flows in the Western Indian Ocean Region. UNEP.

J. Vos. 2020. Ecological flows are exclusionary, technocratic and top-down practices (but could be empowering). Online discussions and debates around water. The Water Alternatives Forum.

Wildlands. 2021. Preliminary aquatic ecology assessment for the Brenwe Hydropower Project, Malekula, Vanuatu: aquatic habitats and species.

B. K. Williams. 2011. Adaptive management of natural resources- framework and issues. *Journal of Environmental Management. 92 (5). pp. 1346-1353.*

World Bank Group (WBG). *2016.* Environmental and Social Framework.

WBG. 2018. Good Practice Handbook: EFlows Assessments for hydropower projects.

World Commission on Dams (WCD). 2000. Dams and Development a New Framework for Decision-Making. The Report of the World Commission on Dams. Earthscan Publications; Thanet Press.

World Wide Fund for Nature (WWF). 2011. Securing environmental flows in the Athabasca River.

WWF. 2017. Listen to the river: Lessons from a global review of Environmental Flows success stories. WWF-UK.

WWF and Lake Victoria Basin Commission. 2010. Final evaluation report. WWF Mara River Basin Management Initiative, Tanzania and Kenya.

H. Zhang et al. 2016. Variation in ecological flow regimes and their response to dams in the upper Yellow River basin. *Environmental Earth Science.* 75 (938).

Environmental Flows Assessment and Management for ADB-Financed Projects

Good Practice Note

This Good Practice Note provides guidance on assessing and managing environmental flows (EFlows) in Asian Development Bank–financed projects. It explains the importance of maintaining the quantity, timing, and quality of water, sediment, and biota flows to sustain healthy rivers, wetlands, and communities. The note outlines step-by-step approaches for integrating EFlows into project planning, design, and monitoring, highlights assessment methods, and emphasizes adaptive management. It presents case studies and best practices to support sustainable development, ecosystem resilience, and compliance with ADB's Environmental and Social Framework.

About the Asian Development Bank

ADB is a leading multilateral development bank supporting inclusive, resilient, and sustainable growth across Asia and the Pacific. Working with its members and partners to solve complex challenges together, ADB harnesses innovative financial tools and strategic partnerships to transform lives, build quality infrastructure, and safeguard our planet. Founded in 1966, ADB is owned by 69 members—50 from the region.

ASIAN DEVELOPMENT BANK
6 ADB Avenue, Mandaluyong City
1550 Metro Manila, Philippines
www.adb.org

www.ingramcontent.com/pod-product-compliance
Lightning Source LLC
Chambersburg PA
CBHW041758220926
51847CB00014B/251
* 9 7 8 9 2 9 2 7 7 6 2 3 7 *